COMPLETELY REVISED AND UPDATED 2ND EDITION

❖ ❖ ❖ ❖ ❖ ❖ ❖ ❖ ❖ ❖ ❖ ❖ ❖ ❖ ❖ ❖ ❖ ❖

SPEAKING
➤ in ➤
TONGUES
A BIBLICAL PERSPECTIVE

❖ ❖ ❖ ❖ ❖ ❖ ❖ ❖ ❖ ❖ ❖ ❖ ❖ ❖ ❖ ❖ ❖ ❖

ROBERT
LINDFELT

D1562562

ACW Press
Phoenix, Arizona 85013

All Scripture cited are from the King James Version as printed in *The Companion Bible*, unless otherwise noted. Explanatory insertions within Scripture verses are enclosed in brackets. All Greek words are transliterated into English and italicized.

Publisher's Cataloging-in-Publication
(*Provided by Quality Books, Inc.*)

Lindfelt, Robert I.
        Speaking in tongues : a biblical perspective / by
Robert I. Lindfelt. -- 1st ed.
        p. cm.
        Includes bibliographical references.
        ISBN 10: 1-892525-85-2
        ISBN 13: 978-1-892525-85-7

        1. Glossolalia--Biblical teaching. 2. Bible. N.T.--
Criticism, interpretation, etc. I. Title.

BS2545.G63L56 2002   234'.132
                QBI02-200416

One of the most misunderstood and underused resources in all Christianity is speaking in tongues.

Contents

PREFACE

JESUS CHRIST PROCLAIMED IT AS A SIGN FOR THOSE WHO would be saved.

It ushered in the Church age that started on the day of Pentecost.

It was the one demonstrative evidence proclaimed in the book of Acts to prove to people that they were born again of God's spirit.

The Scripture encourages everyone to do it and commands that no one forbid it.

And yet, speaking in tongues is perhaps the most misunderstood and underused resource in all of Christianity. Much of the Christian church treats speaking in tongues as some insignificant by-product of offbeat Christianity.

The purpose of this book is to take an honest and open look at speaking in tongues from a biblical perspective.

Although many definitions and explanations exist regarding speaking in tongues, the intent of this work is to gain a precise biblical understanding. God did not supply us with a dictionary of biblical terms so we could simply look up "speaking in tongues" and get an exact understanding. Therefore, we need to investigate the Scriptures so we can get that understanding.

A vital part of this presentation is the survey of twenty-one different records in God's Word that obviously deal with speaking in tongues. Each record is scrutinized to see exactly what speaking in tongues is from a biblical perspective. Other Scriptures pertaining to the subject are also considered to complete this study.

My interest in speaking in tongues came by way of my hunger to know God. My search into spiritual matters started in earnest when I was twelve years old. Although I was exposed to Christianity growing up, it was not a major issue in my life. As I grew older, I investigated many different philosophies and religions. As I concentrated on Christian groups, it was difficult to wade through the many variations of what they proclaimed to be truth. But in spite of the variety of beliefs, a common thread was evident: the Bible. They all recognized the authority of the Bible as the source of truth. So it was here that I focused my endeavors, to find out exactly what the Bible said about God and what He made available to man. It soon became obvious that the integrity of God's Word, and not the various interpretations by man, was what mattered. Thanks to a number of events and some wonderful people dedicated to being workmen of the Word, my understanding of God and His will became more and more meaningful.

One aspect of God's Word that caught my attention was the subject of speaking in tongues. In most Christian circles, speaking in tongues was looked down upon either as unavailable in the present day or as unimportant. But a simple reading of the Scriptures revealed a significant emphasis on speaking in tongues. Speaking in tongues, I discovered, was an essential aspect of the Christian church that God instituted to bless man. It confirmed God's desire for us to know our spiritual relationship with Him.

I first spoke in tongues in 1967 when I was twenty years old, and since that time speaking in tongues has become, and still is, a significant part of my Christian life. Speaking in tongues provides me with unspeakable joy, knowing I have a perfect twenty-four-hour link with my heavenly Father. It has truly given rest to my soul and an assurance to my heart. It confirms the eternal reality of Christ within.

I believe speaking in tongues offers unlimited satisfaction to the heart and soul of every believer who really wants to know the truth of God's purpose. I believe speaking in tongues is one of those undiscovered blessings that have been hidden for too long from most of God's people.

For thirty years, I have dedicated my life to biblical research and Christian service. This book is a continuation of my desire to help people with this dynamic manifestation by opening the Scriptures. I believe anyone who desires to learn can go through the Scriptures carefully and identify what God has purposed for speaking in tongues. I also believe it is available for all believers to experience the many benefits that are derived from speaking in tongues. A wonderful joy awaits the discerning believer as he or she learns about speaking in tongues from the Scriptures.

New 2nd Edition

There are some important reasons why I am expanding the second edition with additional material. One reason is that I have received many favorable responses through the years about the book. Just a few weeks ago, I was blessed to receive the following response: "Recently, my wife ministered to a 69-year-old believer who wanted to know the truth about speaking in tongues. He read the book and was convinced and has manifested!"

Another reason for an expanded second edition is that I wanted to add some additional material that I felt would really complete the full handling of this vital subject. There are three significant chapters added: The Magnificence of Speaking in Tongues, Common Misconceptions and Fears about Speaking in Tongues, and The Benefits of Speaking in Tongues. I have also added some additional material to existing chapters and made a few corrections to grammar.

My goal is to continue providing a biblical source of truth on speaking in tongues. There is still so little written on this subject, though the interest in the manifestations of holy spirit is increasing. Another encouraging note came from a minister from the United Kingdom. He wrote: "Thank you for a real breath of spiritual fresh air in this subject. I pray that you will continue with your courageous attempts to bring the light and truth into the area of the spiritual gifts." I was very touched by his letter.

I pray this new edition will continue moving forward on this most honorable cause of revealing the magnificence of speaking in tongues.

Why a Book on Speaking in Tongues?

FOR A VAST MAJORITY OF CHRISTIANS TODAY, THE MANIFES-tation of speaking in tongues is mostly misunderstood or ignored. Most dismiss it as insignificant or nonexistent. However, the Word of God reveals quite the contrary, as we shall see throughout this study.

God's salvation plan by way of His Son, the Lord Jesus Christ, is the major focus of Christian concern. As a result, much has been written over the centuries about man's redemption through Jesus Christ's life, death, and resurrection. But there is one indispensable aspect of salvation that came with the gift of holy spirit on the day of Pentecost about which little is written and less is understood by most Christians: speaking in tongues.

The Lord Jesus Christ himself said that speaking in tongues would be a sign to those who were saved. Not long after, God's chosen apostles all spoke in tongues when they received the gift of holy spirit for the first time on the day of Pentecost. The fact that God chose speaking in tongues to be the evidence of someone receiving the new birth spirit speaks loudly. The early church recognized the importance of speaking in tongues, as recorded in the book of Acts. The apostle Paul devoted a whole section of Corinthians to the important topic of speaking in tongues. So there is much for the student of the Bible to discover.

What is alarming, however, is that very little has been written about speaking in tongues from a biblical perspective. Books on the subject are virtually nonexistent in regular bookstores, and very little can be found in Christian bookstores. Those books which are available are many times just reprints of works done back in the 1960s and 1970s. Speaking in tongues is a vital enough subject that it needs a new look, and it deserves to be evaluated carefully by investigating the Scriptures.

How do we know if God designed speaking in tongues for every Christian believer? How do we know whether it is a gift, intended for just a few, or a manifestation, intended to show forth the gift? How do we know whether speaking in tongues was intended only for the first century church, or available today as well? This study will address these and other questions.

The purpose of this work is to give each reader, regardless of background, a greater insight and appreciation of the manifestation of speaking in tongues that God designed for man's blessing. This document is not intended to be an exhaustive study of speaking in tongues, but presents a simple foundation of information that allows the Word of God to speak to the reader. This study is intended to help open the door of understanding to those seeking to learn about speaking in tongues— and enjoy the many blessings it brings.

THE DESIGN OF THE BOOK

Chapter 1 asks the pertinent question, "Why a Biblical Perspective?" We live in a society that thrives on having different opinions on things. On this all-important subject, we should not be interested in opinions—yours or mine—but rather what does the Word of God say?

Chapter 2 is vital because if we are going to rely on the Scriptures to provide us answers, then we are going to need to have "Standards for a Workman of God's Word." We will utilize God's standards for being a workman of His Word to rightly divide His Word.

Chapter 3 asks "Why Take the Time to Investigate Speaking in Tongues?" When you discover the significance of speaking in tongues, you will be grateful for the time invested.

The heart of this project is chapter 4, "Twenty-one Records in the Bible on Speaking in Tongues." This is a detailed and methodical investigation of twenty-one records that obviously deal with speaking in tongues. Each record is surveyed carefully to allow the Scriptures to speak for themselves.

After surveying these accounts, a summary of the findings are listed in chapter 5, "The Results of the Survey: Exactly What Is Speaking in Tongues, Its Significance and Benefits." Here we observe the many truths that are revealed from God's Word pertaining to speaking in tongues. We also observe its significance and identify its benefits.

Chapter 6, "Other Scriptures Pertaining to Speaking in Tongues," covers other records that indicate or imply the usage of speaking in tongues that are not covered in the survey of the twenty-one records listed in chapter 4.

Chapter 7, "The Magnificence of Speaking in Tongues," presents a variety of experiences that share the spectacular beauty of speaking in tongues.

Chapter 8, "Common Misconceptions and Fears about Speaking in Tongues," is a careful investigation of God's Word that should eliminate any concerns anyone might have about speaking in tongues.

Chapter 9, "The Benefits of Speaking in Tongues," identifies two of the Bible's most noble men of God who benefitted immensely by speaking in tongues. Also in this chapter is a list of the many wonderful benefits afforded the believer who speaks in tongues.

Chapter 10, "How to Speak in Tongues," is designed to simply and clearly help anyone who desires to speak in tongues to do so.

Chapter 11, closes with "Some Final Words."

In the back of the book are the Acknowledgments and the Bibliography.

I have capitalized "Spirit," "Holy Spirit," and "Holy Ghost" to signify God and put the small case letters for "spirit," "holy spirit," and "holy ghost" to signify the gift which is holy spirit. The KJV Scripture quotes do not reflect this as they are left in their original form.

I trust this work will be a glory to God and the integrity of His Word. I also pray that it will be an opportunity for the reader to partake of something special that God has designed to be a significant blessing in every believer's life.

CHAPTER ONE

Why a Biblical Perspective?

THE BIBLE IS THE WORD OF GOD. IT IS THE OASIS IN MAN'S search for answers through life's desert of existence. It is the final resting place for man's quest for truth.

What is truth? Pilate asked that question of Jesus Christ during Christ's trial, and men have been asking it ever since. While some have remained ignorant, others have tended to pride themselves on their intellect and ability to make up answers to life's challenging questions. Man's intellectual resources appear vast and while he may have the ability to learn, without the Scriptures he is still left without truth. He falls prey to a host of theories that leave him wanting. Unless he turns to and focuses on the Bible, God's Word, man's hunger will remain unsatisfied. The source of truth is simple—God's Word.

John 17:17:
Sanctify them through Thy truth; thy word is truth.

Men's opinions come and go, but truth is eternal. It is reliable.

Deuteronomy 32:3b,4:
…Ascribe ye greatness unto our God.
He is the Rock, His work *is* perfect: For all His ways
are judgment: A GOD of truth and without iniquity,
Just and right *is* He.

II Samuel 22:31:
As for GOD, His way *is* perfect; The word of the
LORD *is* tried: He *is* a buckler to all them that trust
in Him.

The serious seeker will always demand truth. It is truth that makes men and women free.

John 8:32:
And ye shall know the truth, and the truth shall make
you free.

Psalm 19:7:
The law of the LORD *is* perfect, converting the soul:
The testimony of the LORD *is* sure, making wise the
simple.

After researching the subject, I have discovered that writers vary in their conclusions about speaking in tongues. Although most use Scriptures to support their evidence, their discoveries are vastly different. Many question the availability of speaking in tongues today. Other authors say it was just for the early church. Others indicate that it is of little value, while still others state that speaking in tongues is for just a chosen few. These contrary explanations indicate that opinions rather than the truth have been magnified. Truth does not contradict itself.

Then what is the truth? What did God intend when He said, "I would that ye all spake with tongues?" (I Corinthians 14:5).

I hope the hungry soul who is searching for the truth asks, "What does God's Word say? What is God's purpose for speaking in tongues?"

The Scriptures give the true and right perspective on any subject, including speaking in tongues. Man's principal challenge is to search the Scriptures.

> John 5:39:
> Search the scriptures; for in them ye think ye have
> eternal life: and they are they which testify of me.

If we cannot trust God's Word, then what can we trust? It behooves us to come meekly to the Word of God for answers. We can learn to carefully study the Bible, letting God's Word speak for itself. As we concern ourselves with handling the Scriptures with care, we can grow in our knowledge and application of God's Word. If we succumb to following the ignorance of others, we will continue to walk in darkness. Let's rise to the challenge of searching the Scriptures and thereby gain the benefits from the wisdom God promises.

> Proverbs 4:5-7:
> Get wisdom, get understanding: Forget *it* not; neither
> decline from the words of my mouth.
> Forsake her not, and she shall preserve thee: Love her,
> and she shall keep thee.
> Wisdom *is* the principal thing; *therefore* get wisdom:
> And with all thy getting get understanding.

CHAPTER TWO

Standards for a Workman of God's Word

IF WE TRULY DESIRE TO KNOW ABOUT SPEAKING IN TONGUES, then our efforts must be focused on the standard of truth—God's Word. We must approach the Scriptures properly if we expect genuine results. A proper attitude and direction set by God in working and searching His Word is declared in II Timothy 2:15.

> II Timothy 2:15:
> Study to shew thyself approved unto God, a workman that needeth not to be ashamed, rightly dividing the word of truth.

The words "rightly divide" are translated from the Greek word *orthotomounta* which in the New Testament is used exclusively in II Timothy 2:15. It is derived from a combination of two words: *orthos*, which means "correct, straight, or proper," and *temnō*, which means "to cut." In other words, there is a correct or proper way to "cut" the Word of Truth. Man is not to cut up the Word of Truth any way he pleases. He needs to be a workman who studies, cutting the Word properly and correctly.

As a workman digs into the treasures of God's Word with the attitude of rightly dividing the Word of Truth, he needs to be aware of important standards for ascertaining truth provided in the Scriptures. Some of the essential standards we will utilize are as follows:

1. God's Word is not to be privately interpreted.

> II Peter 1:20:
> Knowing this first, that no prophecy of the Scripture is of any private [*idios*, which means "one's own"] interpretation.

This means you and I do not have the privilege of determining the meaning of Scripture. We have to find out what God intended for that Scripture to say. So many times we have our own interpretation of what we think the Bible says. This is evident in the many different opinions concerning speaking in tongues. The first thing we need to understand as workmen of the Word is that we do not privately interpret the meaning of God's Word.

2. God's rightly divided Word cannot contradict itself.

> II Timothy 3:16a:
> All Scripture *is* given by inspiration of God [or, as the Greek text literally says, "God breathed." It is essential that we realize that the Scripture is God's Word].

Since God is perfect, as we have already seen, then His Word has to be perfect. Therefore, there can be no contradictions. If there is an apparent contradiction, then it is probably in our understanding or, perhaps, an error in translation.

II Timothy 3:17 states that the purpose of the God-breathed Word is "that the man of God may be perfect, throughly furnished unto all good works." Thus, it is available to work the integrity of God's Word to find the truth and get its perspective on the subject of speaking in tongues.

3. The context of a section of Scripture must be considered.

We cannot lift a verse out of the context of God's intended meaning. That would be private interpretation rather than allowing the Word of God to interpret itself. Many times verses are taken out of their intended Scriptural use and mutated to teach some other subject according to the teacher's desire. Considering the context of a section of Scripture will be important as we investigate what the Scriptures say about speaking in tongues. When we look at the records in the book of Acts, we will need to be aware of the context of the event that contains speaking in tongues. In I Corinthians chapters 12, 13 and 14, we need to be careful to see the context and not haphazardly make interpretations of one or two isolated verses.

4. Investigation of every occurrence of a word or phrase is important in arriving at the proper biblical understanding of its meaning.

God, like any author, may repeat in varied forms His own previously written or spoken words. He may use different words and combinations of words if He chooses. When He repeats words and phrases, using them in different places under different circumstances, it behooves the workman of the Word to study each occurrence where the same word or phrases appears. By investigating each occurrence, the workman can better understand the precise meaning and garner the wealth of information God has revealed. By following a word or phrase through every occurrence, we can allow the Scripture to define its own words and interpret itself.

These basic standards will help us accurately investigate the crucial subject of speaking in tongues. Our diligent effort in this endeavor is to be workmen, rightly dividing the Word of Truth. The valuable time spent in working the Scriptures will be most rewarding.

CHAPTER THREE

Why Take the Time to Investigate Speaking in Tongues?

THERE ARE SEVERAL IMPORTANT POINTS IN GOD'S WORD that should have arrested our attention to investigate the Scriptures about speaking in tongues.

Of all the things God could have chosen to introduce the gift of holy spirit on the day of Pentecost, He chose speaking in tongues. The fact that all the apostles were operating this new manifestation confirmed that they had received the wonderful power from on high, which was the promise of the Father.

How do we know it was the promise of the Father? Before his ascension, Jesus Christ had told the apostles that he would send the "promise of my Father," and told them to tarry in Jerusalem until they "be endued with power from on high," as recorded in Luke 24:49. He also spoke of signs that would indicate the results of people being saved, such as "they shall speak with new tongues" (Mark 16:17). In Acts, Jesus Christ commanded them "...not to depart from Jerusalem, but wait for the promise of the Father" (Acts 1:4). He then declared that they would "be baptized with the Holy Ghost not many days hence" (Acts 1:5). Just before he ascended, his last words included, "But ye shall receive power, after that the Holy Ghost is come upon you..." (Acts 1:8). So this very important result of the accomplished works of Jesus Christ—the giving of the gift of holy spirit—was marked by the manifestation of speaking in tongues.

> Acts 2:4:
> And they were all filled with the Holy Ghost, and
> began to speak with other tongues, as the Spirit gave
> them utterance.

The events God had recorded about the growth of the early church in Acts describe the importance of speaking in tongues as an indicator to the new Christians that they truly did receive the gift of holy spirit in the new birth. For example, when the Gentiles first received the gift of holy spirit, as recorded in Acts chapter 10, they spoke in tongues. Peter and the other Judeans were astonished when this occurred, because in the culture of the times, it was unheard of that the Gentiles could partake of the things of God. The one act that convinced them that the Gentiles truly had received God's promise was that they heard the Gentiles speak in tongues.

> Acts 10:45,46a:
> And they of the circumcision [a term pertaining to
> Judeans] which believed were astonished, as many
> as came with Peter, because that on the Gentiles also
> was poured out the gift of the Holy Ghost.
> For they heard them speak with tongues, and magnify
> God...

On another occasion, Paul was visiting Ephesus and talking to believers that were earlier taught by Apollos, as recorded in chapter 18. Apollos was an "eloquent man" (Acts 18:24), but when he taught the Ephesians he knew "only the baptism of John" (Acts 18:25). Coming to the area after Apollos left, Paul taught them about Jesus Christ and ministered to them with the result that "the Holy Ghost came on them, and they spake with tongues, and prophesied" (Acts 19:6b). Again, the significance of speaking in tongues was evident.

In addition, there are a number of pointed statements in the book of I Corinthians on the subject of speaking in tongues. These should arrest our attention regarding the significance of speaking in tongues. For God to explain and give details regarding speaking in tongues and other spiritual matters is important to recognize. Some of these points in Corinthians are:

- "But the manifestation of the Spirit is given to every man to profit withal" (I Corinthians 12:7). Speaking in tongues is one of nine manifestations of the Spirit by which man is intended to profit.
- "For he that speaketh in an *unknown* tongue speaketh not unto men, but unto God…" (I Corinthians 14:2). To speak in tongues is to speak to God. What a privilege!
- "He that speaketh in an *unknown* tongue edifieth himself…" (I Corinthians 14:4). Speaking in tongues edifies, or builds up, the speaker.
- "I thank my God, I speak with tongues more than ye all" (I Corinthians 14:18). If the apostle Paul, who is speaking in this verse, spoke in tongues much, perhaps we should as well.
- "…and forbid not to speak with tongues" (I Corinthians 14:39b). Unfortunately, in many churches Christians are advised not to speak in tongues. The Scripture says that it should not be forbidden. God must be in favor of it since the Scripture is God's Word.

As we have observed in the above Scriptures, speaking in tongues is a dynamic subject worth pursuing. The next step is to carefully survey the Scriptures that obviously deal with speaking in tongues. This approach will allow us to see exactly what the Word of God says.

CHAPTER FOUR

Twenty-one Records in the Bible on Speaking in Tongues

INTRODUCTION: COLLECTING INFORMATION ON SPEAKING IN TONGUES

ALTHOUGH MANY DEFINITIONS AND EXPLANATIONS EXIST regarding speaking in tongues, the intent of this work is to gain a precise biblical perspective. Let's go to God's Word and see what God Almighty says.

God did not supply us with a dictionary of biblical terms so we could simply look up "speaking in tongues" and get an exact understanding. Hence, we need to investigate the Scriptures as workmen, rightly dividing the Word of Truth, in order to see exactly what speaking in tongues is.

Using the sequential order of the New Testament books, we will take a careful look at the twenty-one different records that are obviously dealing with speaking in tongues. The structure of the survey is to first quote the particular verse(s), then list key words in the verse with their definitions. To aid our investigation, Greek texts and lexicons have been used to gain more specific definitions of these key words. The basic root word in the Greek will be given for the words we are investigating. Next will be an observation and explanation of what we saw in that particular record.

We will collect as much information as we can from these twenty-one records and then compile it at the end. In doing this, we will scrutinize each section of Scripture.

Survey of the Scriptures

1. **Mark 16:17: "And these signs shall follow them that believe ... they shall speak with new tongues."**

   speak - *laleō*: To talk, speak, tell (Y*). To employ the organ of utterance, to utter words of any language, independently of any reason why they are uttered. To use human voice with words (B).

   new - *kainos*: New, fresh, recent (Y). New, as coming in the place of a thing that was formerly, and as not yet used (B).

   tongues - *glōssa*: A tongue, language (Y).

This verse was spoken by Jesus Christ to his disciples after his resurrection and before his ascension (v.14). The context of

---

* The sources used to define the key words are indicated in parentheses, using capital letters to identify the source. Sources used for defining the words were as follows:

  (Y) - *Young's Analytical Concordance to the Bible*

  (S) - *Strong's Exhaustive Concordance of the Bible*

  (B) - Bullinger's *A Critical Lexicon and Concordance to the English and Greek New Testament*

  (WS) - *The Word Study New Testament* edited by Ralph Winter and Roberta Winter, and (I) - *The Interlinear Literal Translation of the Greek New Testament* by George R. Berry. These resources are the more familiar references in the field of biblical study

this Scripture deals with Jesus Christ teaching his disciples what they were to do in the near future. He was exhorting the apostles to "Go ye into all the world, and preach the gospel…" (v.15). The result would be, "he that believeth and is baptized shall be saved…" (v.16), and "these signs shall follow them that believe" (v.17). The signs would include casting out devils and speaking "with new tongues," (v.17) as well as other signs (v.18). So to "speak with new tongues" was to be a sign.

What is it to "speak with new tongues"? According to the definition of the Greek words used in the texts, it is talking or employing the organ of utterance to speak words of a language that is new or has not yet been used by the speaker.

Thus, we have observed that at a time in the future, as the gospel was being preached, those who would believe and be saved would have signs or indicators of this occurring. One of the signs was going to be that they would speak a language new to them.

2. **Acts 2:4: "And they were all filled with the Holy Ghost, and began to speak with other tongues, as the Spirit gave them utterance."**

Holy Ghost - *pneuma hagion*: separate, set apart (Y). *pneuma*: The wind, the breath breathed forth, the element of life (B). The terms "Holy Ghost" or "Holy Spirit" are both translated from the same Greek words, *pneuma hagion*. Most of the time the words used together refer either to God, the Giver, who is the Holy Spirit, or His gift, which is holy spirit, given first on the day of Pentecost.

to speak - *laleō*: See # 1.

other - *heteros*: Other, different (Y). Other, denoting generic distinction (B).

tongues - *glōssa*: See # 1.

as - *kathos*: According as (B).

the Spirit - *pneuma*: Breathing as the sign and condition of life, breath. That which cannot be apprehended by the

senses, but is recognized only by its operation or manifestations, as it is seen in life (B).

gave - *didomi*: To give with implied notion of giving freely,
unforced (B).

utterance - *apophthengomai*: To speak out, utter aloud (B).

This event recorded in Acts 2:4 occurred on the day of
Pentecost. It was the fulfillment of the promise of the gift of holy
spirit that Jesus Christ had spoken about in Acts 1:8, "But ye
shall receive power, after that the Holy Ghost is come upon you:
and ye shall be witnesses unto me…."

The giving of holy spirit as recorded in Acts 2:4 was the cul-
mination of what Jesus Christ had emphasized to his apostles
before his death, as well as in his resurrected body prior to his
ascension (Before his death: See John 7:38,39; 14:16,17,25,26;
15:26,27; and 16:7. After his resurrection and before his ascension: See Luke 24:49; John 20:22, and Acts 1:4-9.).

On the day of Pentecost, God chose to give the gift of holy
spirit. He filled the apostles with holy spirit and they began to
speak, utter, a different language as God, who is Spirit, gave them
utterance. We also observe that they were not being forced to
speak. They, by their freedom of will, spoke.

Remember in the first record, Mark 16:17, we learned that
"speak[ing] with new tongues" would be a sign following those
who believed to be saved. We see this clearly in this account, and
we will see it develop further in subsequent records.

3. **Acts 2:11: "Cretes and Arabians, we do hear them speak
   in our tongues the wonderful works of God."**

   hear - *akouō*: To perceive with the ears. To hear (B).

   speak - *laleō*: See # 1.

   our - *heemeteros*: Our own (B).

   tongues - *glōssa*: See # 1.

   wonderful works - *megalia*: Great, grand, magnificent (B).

   God - *Theos*: God (Y).

This is still the day of Pentecost. People from many nations were hearing tongues being spoken for the first time. When the integrity of God's Word is worked to the end it is rightly divided, we see that these events of Pentecost did not take place in an upper room, but in "the house" of God, the Temple, where all could witness this amazing event. The people listening to the apostles speaking in tongues heard their own languages (v.6). They were amazed that Galileans could speak these different foreign languages because, according to the culture of the times, Galileans were looked down upon by Judeans and others as ignorant and unlearned (v.7). These people from different nations heard their languages being spoken, and what they heard in their languages were the wonderful works of God. Evidently, when someone speaks in tongues he may be speaking in a known language and, according to the Scriptures, he speaks the wonderful works of God.

4. **Acts 2:33: "Therefore being by the right hand of God exalted, and having received of the Father the promise of the Holy Ghost, He hath shed forth this, which *ye* now see and hear."**
   shed forth - *ekcheō*: To pour out (B).
   see - *blepō*: To look at, observe (B).
   hear - *akouō*: To give ear, hear (Y).

Peter, teaching the people on this eventful day of Pentecost, explained what was going on. He referred to the evidence of the receiving of the gift of holy spirit from the Father as "that which they saw and heard." Speaking in tongues was what they saw and heard. It was the evidence of the reality of the receiving of holy spirit by the apostles.

5. **Acts 10:45,46: "And they of the circumcision which believed were astonished, as many as came with Peter, because that on the Gentiles also was poured out the**

gift of the Holy Ghost. For they heard them speak with tongues, and magnify God…"

speak - *laleō*: See # 1.

tongues - *glōssa*: See # 1.

magnify - *megalunō*: To make great (Y).

The context of this record deals with the conversion of Cornelius, the centurion, in Caesarea. God worked diligently with Peter to get him to realize that the new birth, which was first made available on the day of Pentecost, was also available to the Gentiles. Before the day of Pentecost, God's relationship had already been established with the children of Israel. Now Peter was learning that God had opened the door of salvation to all people.

This section of Scripture clearly and distinctly declares that speaking in tongues was the undisputed evidence that someone had received the gift of holy spirit. Chapter 10 unfolds in detail the account of the Gentiles first receiving the new birth. Evidently the only proof satisfactory to Peter and other Judeans ("they of the circumcision") that came with Peter was that they heard the Gentiles speak in tongues. The Scriptures said that they were "astonished" because they could not believe that the Gentiles were allowed to receive the new birth. It took the proof of speaking in tongues to convince those skeptical Judeans. Another point to observe in this Scripture is that when the Gentiles spoke in tongues they were magnifying God.

Later (in chapter 11) when the "apostles and brethren" in Judea heard that "the Gentiles had also received the word of God," they "contended" with Peter. Peter explained how he learned that God had opened salvation to the Gentiles. Peter, dealing with the elders in Jerusalem, declared, "And as I began to speak, the holy ghost fell on them, as on us at the beginning" (Acts 11:15). The evidence of the holy ghost falling on them could only have been the act of speaking in tongues which had occurred on the day of Pentecost, "at the beginning."

6. Acts 19:6: "And when Paul had laid *his* hands upon them, the Holy Ghost came on them; and they spake with tongues, and prophesied."

spake - *laleō*: See # 1

tongues - *glōssa*: See # 1

prophesied - *propheetuo⁻*: To publicly expound (Y). A speaking forth (B). In most people's minds, this word means to "foretell the future." Biblically, it can mean to foretell the future or merely to speak forth or expound something.

It is important to realize the context in which this occurred. We need to start in Acts 18:24 and read through Acts 19:6 to gain an appreciable background of what was really happening. After reading Acts 18:24 through 19:6, it becomes clear that those to whom Apollos ministered in Ephesus had limited knowledge regarding salvation. In spite of being a dynamic speaker, Apollos did not know about the new birth salvation; he only knew "the baptism of John." Then Aquilla and Priscilla took Apollos aside and "expounded unto him the way of God more perfectly" (Acts 18:26). When Paul came into town later, he quickly realized that something was lacking. Paul then ministered to the new Ephesian believers (by laying on of hands) and the gift of holy spirit came upon them in manifestation by way of speaking in tongues and prophesy.

We see again that speaking in tongues was the evidence that showed Paul that these people had received the gift of holy spirit. As a result of the limited teaching of Apollos, these Ephesians needed more instruction. So when Paul arrived, he ministered to them to the point in which they manifested the gift of holy spirit by speaking in tongues and prophecy. This is the first time we see "prophecy" mentioned. We will learn more of this manifestation later in this study.

7. I Corinthians 12:10: "To another the working of miracles; to another prophecy; to another discerning of

spirits; to another *divers* kinds of tongues; to another the interpretation of tongues:"

prophecy - *propheetia*: See # 6 (From the same root word).

kinds of - *genos*: Race, class, genus (B).

tongues - *glōssa*: See # 1.

interpretation - *hermeneia*: Explanation (Y).

tongues - *glōssa*: See # 1.

The immediate context of this section of Scripture starts with verse 7, "But the manifestation of the Spirit is given to every man to profit withal." A listing of nine manifestations follows, with speaking in tongues listed eighth. The words "to another" are better translated from the Greek as "for another." They refer back to the word "profit" in verse 7, "But the manifestation of the spirit is given to every man to profit withal." Many erroneously think the words "to another" in verse 10 refer to the manifestations being given out to different people, so that some people can do miracles and others speak in tongues, etc. This is contrary to the rest of God's Word, as evidenced in verse 7, "But the manifestation of the spirit is given to <u>every man</u> to profit withal" (emphasis added).

The manifestations in the following verses are so listed to emphasize the profit of each one. When understood literally, the section reads, "to another [profit] working of miracles; to another [profit] prophecy; to another [profit] discerning of spirits; to another [profit] *divers* kinds of tongues; to another [profit] the interpretation of tongues." This fits with the accuracy of God's Word.

Speaking in tongues falls into a list of nine things that are called "manifestations" (v.7). The word "kinds" (v.10) used with speaking in tongues indicates that there is not just one language for speaking in tongues. This was evident on the day of Pentecost when many languages were represented. Prophecy, as we saw in Acts 19:6, is also listed as a manifestation. Another manifestation listed is interpretation of tongues, which will be handled later while dealing with I Corinthians 14.

As we read through I Corinthians 12 carefully, we see that the overall context is "spiritual matters." Some people may have noticed a different term used in the chapter heading of their Bibles, such as "spiritual gifts." The reason for this comes from verse 1, which reads, "Now concerning spiritual *gifts* brethren, I would not have you ignorant." It is important to recognize that the word "gifts" is italicized in the Authorized King James Version. This means that the translators added the word to the text. There is no corresponding Greek word for "gifts." The Greek word for "spiritual" in this verse is *pneumatikos*, meaning, "belonging to the Spirit" (B). With this understanding, this part of the verse could be translated, "concerning things of the Spirit" or "concerning spiritual matters."

Our concern for Scriptural accuracy and integrity needs to be maintained as we work chapter 12. Let's see why this section of Scripture is concerning "spiritual matters" rather than "spiritual gifts." In verse 4, "diversities of gifts" is mentioned, then in verse 5, "differences of administrations"; then in verse 6, "diversities of operations"; and finally, verse 7 states, "But the manifestation of the Spirit is given to every man...." Chapter 12 expounds on many different spiritual matters, not just "spiritual gifts."

As we take the time to explore the biblical usage of words, we see that although many people refer to speaking in tongues as a spiritual gift, accurately understood it is one of the nine manifestations of the gift of holy spirit "given to every man to profit withal" (v.7). Calling speaking in tongues a gift infers that God favors some by granting them the privilege to speak in tongues. This is not the case. One of the lessons Peter and the others with him had learned in hearing the Gentiles speak in tongues is recorded in Acts 10:34b: "God is no respecter of persons." So God does not select certain people to speak in tongues and others not; it is a manifestation of the spirit that every believer can potentially operate.

Another vital point to recognize is who operates the manifestations of the spirit. Does the person who has the spirit operate it or does the spirit operate the man? It has been clear in all the previous verses we have examined that the people spoke in tongues by their freedom of will. There is no indication they were forced or controlled.

I Corinthains 12:11 also answers the question of who operates the manifestations: "But all these worketh that one and the selfsame Spirit dividing to every man severally as he wills." Some Bibles capitalize the word "he" to make it seem that God does the initiating. The Greek manuscripts do not capitalize this word and the translations should read, "...as he [the individual person] wills." This is in agreement with all the other records we have studied. It certainly fits with verse 7, which introduces the subject of the manifestations, "But the manifestation of the Spirit is given to every man to profit withal."

8. **I Corinthians 12:28-30: "And God hath set some in the church, first apostles, secondarily prophets, thirdly teachers, after that miracles, then gifts of healings, helps, governments, diversities of tongues. *Are* all apostles? *Are* all prophets? *Are* all teachers? *Are* all workers of miracles? Have all the gifts of healing? Do all speak with tongues? Do all interpret?"**

   diversities - *genos*: See # 7, the same word as "kinds."

   tongues - *glōssa*: See # 1.

Remember, the overall context of this chapter deals with spiritual matters functioning properly in the church. Verse 28 is a list of a few things God has set in the church. In verses 29 and 30 a series of rhetorical questions are asked for emphasis. Do all believers function by doing all of these things? No! Some specialize at doing one or some of these. Again, the proper functioning of all the spiritual matters within the church is important. This includes gift ministries, the proper operation of the manifestations, and other services to bless the body of Christ.

Speaking in tongues along with other spiritual matters (gift ministries, helps, etc.) are listed to make the desired point: All these aspects are important to the operation of the church. God purposely set speaking in tongues—along with the other important things that are listed—in the church to be a significant part of the functioning of the body of Christ.

There is an important note that should be made at this point. I Corinthians 12:31, which follows the above record, says, "But covet earnestly the best gifts: and yet shew I unto you a more excellent way." This verse sets up Chapter 13 to tell us the more excellent way than coveting, which is the love of God in operation. But a point may be made that in the first part of the verse the word "gifts" is used to describe all the things listed above it, including speaking in tongues. The Greek word for gift in this verse is *charisma* which means, "a gift of grace, a free gift" (B). Certainly it is by God's grace we have all those things mentioned and much more. Speaking in tongues and the other manifestations, as well as the ministries listed, are by God's grace and freely given. Everyone born again of God's spirit has the potential to operate the nine manifestations. It is truly a gift of grace to be able to do this.

9. **I Corinthians 13:1,2: "Though I speak with the tongues of men and of angels, and have not charity, I am become as sounding brass, or a tinkling cymbal. And though I have *the gift* of prophecy, and understand all mysteries, and all knowledge; and though I have all faith, so that I could remove mountains, and have not charity, I am nothing."**

   speak - *laleō*: See # 1.

   tongues - *glōssa*: See # 1.

   angels - *angelos*: One who is sent in order to announce, teach, or perform anything (B).

   charity - *agapē*: Love from God (Y).

   The context of this chapter is the answer to the previous verse (12:31), showing unto the reader "a more excellent way" than coveting. The "more excellent way" is the love of God.

God is evidently emphasizing the importance of His love in operation by contrasting it to a number of other worthy spiritual actions. These worthy spiritual actions are: first, speaking in tongues; next, prophecy; then, understanding mysteries and having all knowledge; and finally, having faith to remove mountains. This is quite a notable list! Many people use verse one to say how unimportant speaking in tongues is. Yet, when we observe the company it keeps with the other qualities listed, suddenly speaking in tongues is highly recognized. It is the first item to be used to highlight the love of God in operation.

It is important to note that verse one says, "speak with the tongues of men and of angels." This indicates that when someone speaks in tongues, the tongue must be a language of men or of angels.

10. I Corinthians 13:8: "Charity never faileth: but whether *there be* **prophecies, they shall fail; whether** *there be* **tongues, they shall cease; whether** *there be* **knowledge, it shall vanish away."**

charity - *agapē*: See # 9.
prophecies - *propheetia*: See # 6.
tongues - *glōssa*: See # 1.

The love of God in operation is again being emphasized in this chapter. To understand this verse, we need to read the next two verses: "For we know in part, and we prophesy in part. But when that which is perfect is come, then that which is in part shall be done away" (I Corinthians 13:9,10). Basically what is being said is that charity will never fail even though these other things will be done away with when the Lord Jesus Christ returns.

The manifestation of speaking in tongues is used along with other manifestations to illustrate a point. The point is that "charity," the love of God, will never cease even when "that which is perfect is come" (which will happen when Jesus Christ returns). Everything is in "part" until the Lord Jesus Christ returns. At that point, the manifestations will be of no further use, and therefore they will be done away with.

11. **I Corinthians 14:2: "For he that speaketh in an *unknown* tongue speaketh not unto men, but unto God: for no man understandeth *him*; howbeit in the spirit he speaketh mysteries."**

speaketh - *laleō*: (used 3 times) See # 1.

tongue - *glōssa*: See # 1.

understand - *akouo*: To hear, to perceive with the ears (B). This Greek word is used 437 times in the Bible and is usually translated "hear."

mysteries - *musterion*: A sacred secret (B).

Chapter 14 deals extensively with the manifestations of speaking in tongues, interpretation of tongues, and prophecy, and how they are to be used in the church.

The word "unknown" is italicized in the Authorized King James Version, which means it was added to the text by the translators. We have already observed that speaking in tongues is a language of men or angels (See # 3, Acts 2:11, and # 9, I Corinthians 13:1). Although new or unknown to the speaker, the language could possibly be recognized by someone else.

This Scripture states that when a person is speaking in tongues, that person is speaking to God, not men. What a wonderful means of communication with God! People who desire to speak to God can benefit greatly by speaking in tongues.

The verse also declares that when someone speaks in tongues (which is how one speaks "in the spirit"), he is speaking mysteries.

12. **I Corinthians 14:4: "He that speaketh in an *unknown* tongue edifieth himself; but he that prophesieth edifieth the church."**

speaketh -*laleō*: See # 1.

tongue - *glōssa*: See # 1.

edifieth - *oikodomeo*: To build up (Y).
prophesieth - *propheetia*: See # 6.

This verse indicates how the manifestations of speaking in tongues and prophecy are to be used.

God designed speaking in tongues to edify, or build up, the individual speaking. We also see one of the purposes of prophecy, which is to edify, or build up, the church. Speaking in tongues is for the individual believer to build himself up and prophecy is for building up all the believers that are present in that particular fellowship where prophecy is manifested.

13. **I Corinthians 14:5: "I would that ye all spake with tongues, but rather than ye prophesied: for greater is he that prophesieth than he that speaketh with tongues, except he interpret, that the church may receive edifying."**
   spake - *laleō*: See # 1.
   tongues - *glōssa*: See # 1.
   prophesied - *propheetia*: See # 6.
   interpret - *diermeneuo*: To explain thoroughly (Y).
   edifying - *oikodome*: See # 12.

This verse deals with three manifestations and gives us insight on how they are to be used.

God desires that all believers speak in tongues. But in the church, which is the whole body of believers, He prefers the operation of prophecy or interpretation of tongues. Why? Because prophecy and interpretation of tongues are spoken in a language understandable to those in the church. We have already learned that when someone speaks in tongues they speak not unto men but unto God (v.2). The main concern in this verse is "that the church may receive edifying"—the whole church, not the individual.

The purpose of prophecy is also handled in verse 3: "But he that prophesieth speaketh unto men *to* edification, and exhortation, and comfort."

14. **I Corinthians 14:6: "Now, brethren, if I come unto you speaking with tongues, what shall I profit you, except I shall speak to you either by revelation, or by knowledge, or by prophesying or by doctrine."**

speaking - *laleō*: See # 1.

tongues - *glōssa*: See # 1.

revelation - *apokalupsis*: To unveil or uncover (B).

knowledge - *gnosis*: Knowledge acquired by learning or effort (B).

prophesying - *propheetia*: See # 6.

God takes the time in His Word to distinguish between the application of the manifestations of speaking in tongues, interpretation of tongues, and prophecy, which have different functions in the church.

A strong point is being made in this section of Scripture regarding the proper operation of the manifestations of speaking in tongues, interpretation of tongues, and prophecy. It is evident that speaking in tongues is for the "edification" (v.4) of the believer, and the language spoken may not be understood by the hearer(s). Speaking in tongues is designed for an individual's personal prayer life. The manifestations of interpretation of tongues and prophecy are meant to "edify" (v.3,4) the people in the Church. Verses 7-11 are used to emphasize the differences of the operations of these manifestations so that it can be clearly understood that speaking in tongues is not to be done out loud in public meetings unless interpreted.

15. **I Corinthians 14:12,13: "Even so ye, forasmuch as ye are zealous of spiritual *gifts*, seek that ye may excel to the edifying of the church. Wherefore let him that speaketh in an *unknown* tongue pray that he may interpret."**

spiritual - *pneuma*: See # 2.

Edifying - *oikodomeo*: See # 12.

speak - *laleō*: See # 1.

tongues - *glōssa*: See # 1.

pray - *proseuchomai*: To offer prayer or speak out to God (B).

interpret - *diermeneuo*: See # 13.

These verses continue to explain the proper operation of the manifestations of speaking in tongues and the interpretation of tongues. Other people hearing someone speak in tongues are not going to benefit because the speaker is speaking not unto men but unto God (I Corinthians 14:2); he is edifying himself.

Again in verse 12, the word "gifts" is italicized, indicating it was added by the translators. We have seen this several times already with this word.

Those zealous for spiritual things are encouraged to seek that they may "excel to the edifying of the church." For the benefit of the church, the believer who speaks in tongues in the church should be praying to God that he, the same person, may interpret. Why? As we have already seen in verses 5 and 6, so that everyone in the church is edified.

The free will operation of the manifestations by the believers is very evident throughout this chapter and other sections in the Bible. It is obvious that the believer is not being controlled or forced to operate the manifestations of holy spirit; believers use their freedom of will to operate the manifestations. If they operate the manifestations incorrectly, as those in Corinth, they do so by their choice and to their own detriment. This section in I Corinthians (chapters 12, 13, and 14) corrects the misuse of the manifestations along with dealing with other spiritual matters.

16. I Corinthians 14:14-17: "For if I pray in an *unknown* tongue, my spirit prayeth, but my understanding is unfruitful. What is it then? I will pray with the spirit, and I will pray with the understanding also: I will sing with the spirit, and I will sing with the understanding also.

Else when thou shalt bless with the spirit, how shall he that occupieth the room of the unlearned say "Amen" at thy giving of thanks, seeing he understandeth not what thou sayest? For thou verily givest thanks well, but the other is not edified."

pray - *proseuchomai*: See # 15.

spirit - *pneuma*: See # 2.

understand - *nous*: The organ of mental perception and apprehension (B).

sing - *psallo*: To sing praise with a musical instrument (Y).

givest thanks - *eucharisteo*: To show oneself grateful (B).

edified - *oikodome*: See # 12.

The instruction regarding the proper use of speaking in tongues continues.

The italicized word "unknown" in verse 14 was added by the translators, so it is devoid of scriptural authority. As we have seen, speaking in tongues could be a known language.

Speaking in tongues is referred to as an act of prayer in verse 14, "For if I pray in an *unknown* tongue…." It is to "pray with the spirit" (v.15), which can be used as another means of praying besides to "pray with the understanding" (v.15).

It is available to sing in tongues ("sing with the spirit," v.15). What a joy to sing with words that are from God!

Speaking in tongues is referred to as "to bless with the spirit" (v.16). The believer has the privilege and opportunity to bless others by using the spirit via speaking in tongues. We will see later in this study that an aspect of "blessing with the spirit" is to pray for them by speaking in tongues. (see chapter 6: "A Consideration of Other Scriptures Pertaining to Speaking in Tongues," #2.)

Verses 16 and 17 remind believers again that to speak in tongues out loud to a group of other believers is not edifying because people may not understand the language and will not know when to say "amen."

Speaking in tongues is also a means of "giving thanks" as indicated in verses 16 and 17. What an ideal way to extend our gratefulness to the heavenly Father by using the spirit He gave us.

17. I Corinthians 14:18,19: "I thank my God, I speak with tongues more than ye all: Yet in the church I had rather speak five words with my understanding, that *by my voice* I might teach others also, than ten thousand words in an *unknown* tongue."

speak - *laleō*: See # 1.

tongues - *glōssa*: See # 1.

understanding - *nous*: See # 16.

Paul obviously spoke in tongues much, which emphasizes the importance of speaking in tongues. He spoke in tongues more than the Corinthian church. The Corinthians also spoke in tongues, even though out of order many times, as indicated in previous verses.

Here, he was instructing the Corinthians that, although he spoke in tongues much, speaking in tongues out loud in their presence would not be beneficial to them. They would not understand the words spoken in tongues. We have seen this point emphasized previously in I Corinthians chapter 14. The Corinthian church was in dire need of instruction through a known language. They needed to hear Paul's message rather than to hear someone speak in tongues.

18. I Corinthians 14:22,23: "Wherefore tongues are for a sign, not to them that believe, but to them that believe not: but prophesying *serveth* not for them that believe not, but for them which believe. If therefore the whole church be come together into one place, and all speak with tongues, and there come in *those that are* unlearned, or unbelievers, will they not say that ye are mad?"

tongues - *glōssa*: See # 1.

sign - *semeion*: A sign by which any thing is designated, distinguished, or known (B).

prophesy - *propheetia*: See # 6.

Instruction on the proper use of speaking in tongues continues. Speaking in tongues is a sign to unbelievers. They have evidence that something special is happening.

But it is not proper for everyone to come together and speak in tongues, because if there is anyone in that meeting that does not understand, that person is going to hear many different languages being spoken that make no apparent sense. This point has been made before in verses 15-17, but it is taught differently so there will be no misunderstanding regarding the proper use of speaking in tongues.

19. I Corinthians 14:26: "How is it then, brethren? when ye come together, every one of you hath a psalm, hath a doctrine, hath a tongue, hath a revelation, hath an interpretation. Let all things be done unto edifying."

tongue - *glōssa*: See # 1.

revelation - *apokalupsis*: See # 14.

interpretation - *diermeneuo*: See # 13.

The church is being taught how to conduct itself. The Corinthians were evidently not doing things correctly. They clearly had many problems with how they utilized the manifestations, as well as with other spiritual matters. Paul, by revelation from God, reproved and corrected them. It was not proper for everyone to participate selfishly, which included speaking in tongues out of order. What is paramount is that everything be done to edify the church.

20. I Corinthians 14:27: "If any man speak in an *unknown* tongue, *let it be* by two, or at the most *by* three, and *that* by course; and let one interpret."

speak - *laleō*: See # 1.

tongue - *glōssa*: See # 1.

interpret - *diermeneuo*: See # 13.

This verse continues the correction of how spiritual matters are to be conducted in the church by explaining how the manifestation of tongues with interpretation should be operated in the church. The instruction is to have two or three messages through speaking in tongues and interpretation. It is important to understand that in "let one interpret," "one" refers to the same person who speaks in tongues. Many erroneously say that one speaks in tongues and another person interprets. This cannot be right, for verse 5 of this chapter sets the standard for how it is to be done: "…greater *is* he that prophesieth than he that speaketh with tongues, except he [the same person] interpret, that the church may receive edifying."

21. I Corinthians 14:39,40: "Wherefore, brethren, covet to prophesy, and forbid not to speak with tongues. Let all things be done decently and in order."

prophesy - *propheetia*: See # 6.

speak - *laleō*: See # 1.

tongues - *glōssa*: See # 1.

decently - *euschemonos*: Gracefully with dignity (B).

order - *taxis*: A setting in order, arrangement (B).

The instruction to the Corinthians on the proper operation of the manifestations of holy spirit is coming to a close with these last two verses.

After all the reproof and correction in I Corinthians 14, the Corinthians are encouraged to desire the manifestation of prophesy, which we have learned in verses 3 and 4 has the purpose of building up the church by "edification, and exhortation, and comfort."

They are also commanded, "forbid not to speak in tongues." Evidently, God desires that people speak in tongues. It should be extremely clear what God's position is on speaking in tongues. He is highly in favor of it! Why would God devote this much of His Word to the subject of speaking in tongues if it is unimportant?

This last verse tells the believers to operate manifestations in the church with graceful dignity and have an arrangement or order in what they do. The heavenly Father is a God of decency and order. Everything He does—and would have us to do—*must* be decent and in order.

These twenty-one records give an abundance of information on speaking in tongues. They are the very clear and obvious verses that contain biblical instruction regarding speaking in tongues. What follows is a compilation of the information we have seen from these twenty-one records about speaking in tongues.

CHAPTER FIVE

The Results of the Survey: Exactly What Is Speaking in Tongues, Its Significance and Benefits

THE FOLLOWING IS A LISTING OF THE TRUTHS DISCOVERED
from the survey section and a description of what speaking in
tongues is—including its significance and benefits. Because only
the verse references are listed, the reader is encouraged to refer
back to the survey. After the listing of verse references, a further
explanation of each of the points is provided.

1. *Speaking in tongues is a sign indicating that a person is
   saved and filled with the gift of holy spirit, the gift which first
   became available on the day of Pentecost.*
   - Mark 16:15-17
   - Acts 2:4
   - Acts 2:33
   - Acts 10:45,46
   - Acts 19:6
   - Romans 8:16
   - I Corinthians 14:22

The first time speaking in tongues is specifically mentioned is in Mark 16:15-17. The Scriptures declare it to be a sign to identify the saved believer. "And these signs shall follow them that believe…they shall speak with new tongues" (Mark 16:17). Jesus Christ introduced speaking in tongues as the God-chosen means that would in the near future identify a believer as being saved and filled with the gift of holy spirit.

A number of days later, the day of Pentecost ushered in the reality of what Jesus Christ was saying. "And they were all filled with the Holy Ghost, and began to speak with other tongues…" (Acts 2:4). Clearly, here was the sign declared by Jesus Christ indicating they were truly saved and filled with holy spirit.

Speaking in tongues was the confirmation for Peter and the other Judeans of the first Gentiles being born again, as recorded in Acts 10:45,46. "And they of the circumcision which believed were astonished, as many as came with Peter, because that on the Gentiles also was poured out the gift of the Holy Ghost. For they heard them speak with tongues…."

Another record indicating speaking in tongues as a sign of salvation and being filled with the gift of holy spirit is Acts 19:6, "And when Paul had laid his hands upon them, the Holy Ghost came on them; and they spake with tongues…."

God gave man an undeniable, easily recognizable sign by which a man could prove to himself and others that he is born again with the gift of holy spirit. God gave him the wonderful ability to speak in tongues. Speaking in tongues is the indication in the physical realm of the spiritual reality of the presence of the gift of holy spirit born within.

2. *Speaking in tongues is when a saved person utilizes the organs of speech to speak a language that is new or unknown to the speaker. It comes by way of the Spirit who gives the words to utter.*
   + Mark 16:17   + Acts 2:4

This is the physical action that takes place every time someone speaks in tongues. They are verbalizing, speaking audible words, of a language unknown to themselves.

The God-chosen words "speaking in tongues" describes the action of what is happening. A believer speaks words of a language unknown to him or her. Its source is God: "…as the Spirit gave them utterance" (Acts 2:4).

When one speaks in tongues, one utilizes the same organs of speech as he does speaking in English or any other known language. He moves his lips, his mouth, and his throat, he breathes out, and he speaks the words. He does not understand them, but they flow out just like any language being spoken.

3. Speaking in tongues is a language of men or angels.

+ Acts 2:11   + I Corinthians 13:1

On the day of Pentecost, the very first time people spoke in tongues, they spoke languages unknown to them but recognizable to the many foreign visitors who had gathered in Jerusalem, who declared, "…we do hear them speak in our tongues the wonderful works of God" (Acts 2:11).

God declares in I Corinthians 13:1 that when believers speak in tongues it is "the tongues of men and of angels." There are many thousands of languages and dialects spoken around the world. I do not have a clue what angels speak, but evidently it is possible to use their language(s) while speaking in tongues.

4. Speaking in tongues is speaking the wonderful works of God.

+ Acts 2:11

People may inquire about what is being said when someone speaks in tongues. God's Word declares that while they were speaking in tongues on the day of Pentecost, they were speaking the "wonderful works of God" (Acts 2:11). What a privilege to speak the wonderful works of God.

5. *Speaking in tongues magnifies God.*
  + Acts 10:46

According to God's Word, when a believer speaks in tongues he magnifies God.

After reading verses such as this, I am flabbergasted by the comments of Christians who say speaking in tongues has no significance. Is magnifying the heavenly Father not significant? God has done so much for us through His Son Jesus Christ. Can we not utilize the manifestation of the spirit that God designed for us to magnify Him? We should speak in tongues much!

6. *Speaking in tongues is one of the nine manifestations of the gift of holy spirit.*
  + I Corinthians 12:7-10

The list of the nine operations of the spirit are called by God "manifestations." This term indicates that these are evidences of the gift of holy spirit. All nine are available to use so that the believer can walk effectively by the spirit.

7. *Speaking in tongues is done by the free will operation of a believer without being possessed or controlled. In other words, the believer does the speaking, not something forcing or controlling him.*

+ Acts 2:4	+ I Corinthians 14:4
+ Acts 10:45,46	+ I Corinthians 14:5
+ Acts 19:6	+ I Corinthians 14:13
+ I Corinthians 14:2	+ I Corinthians 14:40

God never possesses the believer. Never! Our heavenly Father has given us freedom of will to choose whether to operate the manifestations or not. At all the places where speaking in tongues is mentioned, never is there evidence of God controlling the believer or forcing him.

Of the forty-five years I have spoken in tongues, never have I been possessed or forced by God. The adversary, the devil, will possess and control people if they allow him, but God never does. It is a refreshing sense of freedom that I have when I initiate the action of speaking in tongues. I make the free-will decision to magnify God and speak the wonderful works of God by speaking in tongues, and God is always there to do His part.

Actually it is easier to speak in tongues than to speak in English. Why? Because to speak in English, I have to think about the words I will use. When I speak in tongues, I just speak out the words that are already provided by God.

8. *Speaking in tongues shall cease when "that which is perfect is come," who is the Lord Jesus Christ returning to gather together the saints (I Thessalonians 4:14-18).*
   + I Corinthians 13:8-10

Some teach that speaking in tongues was only available to operate in the early church and is no longer necessary or available. Many of them will quote I Corinthians 13:8, "...whether there be tongues, they shall cease..." as proof of that. Unfortunately, those teachers take this verse out of its context, which includes verse 10, "When that which is perfect is come, then that which is in part shall be done away." When the Lord Jesus Christ returns to gather the church together, then that which is perfect will have come. At that time, we will no longer need speaking in tongues.

9. *Speaking in tongues is speaking to God, not men.*
   + I Corinthians 14:2

This verse clearly and simply declares the magnitude of speaking in tongues and its significance. When you speak in tongues you speak to God, not to men.

Speaking in tongues is the direct access God designed so we could go straight to Him. What a benefit to have this open communication line to God. When I speak in tongues, I know my prayer is going straight to the heavenly Father.

10. *Speaking in tongues is to speak mysteries.*
  + I Corinthians 14:2

God's Word declares that when we speak in tongues we speak mysteries.

11. *Speaking in tongues edifies the speaker.*
  + I Corinthians 14:4

Another benefit to speaking in tongues is that the speaker is built up or edified. "He that speaketh in an *unknown* tongue edifieth himself..." (I Corinthians 14:4).

There have been times in my life that I have been beaten down or discouraged, or times when everything seemed to be going against me. At these times I would speak in tongues and edify myself and be reminded of the spirit of God in me. Speaking in tongues reminds me of the reality that I am a son of God with power. This simple act of speaking in tongues helps me keep in perspective the reality of who I am before God.

12. *Speaking in tongues is for every believer to operate.*
  + I Corinthians 14:5

I Corinthians 14:5 says, "I would that ye all spake with tongues...." This verse also emphasizes the importance of prophecy and tongues with interpretation so that the church may receive edifying. But this does not lessen the will of God for *everyone* to speak in tongues.

13. *A believer who speaks in tongues should also pray and desire to edify the church through interpretation of tongues and prophecy.*
  + I Corinthians 14:12

Although this study focuses on just one of the nine manifestations, learning about the other eight would enrich and fulfill the walk of any Christian believer.

The records in I Corinthians indicate that believers were expected not only to speak in tongues, but also to learn to speak in tongues and interpret and prophesy so they could give messages that would build up those in the church.

14. *Speaking in tongues is praying with the spirit.*
- I Corinthians 14:14   - Jude 20
- Ephesians 6:18

There are two ways to pray. "I will pray with the spirit, and I will pray with the understanding also..." (I Corinthians 14:15). God made it available for us to pray to Him via speaking in tongues (prayer in the spirit) or prayer with our understanding.

The challenge for many is to have a successful prayer life. You can never go wrong praying in the spirit, which is speaking in tongues. "For if I pray in an *unknown* tongue, my spirit prayeth..." (I Corinthians 14:4).

15. *A believer can sing in tongues.*
- I Corinthians 14:15   - Ephesians 5:19

God is blessed with praise in song to Him. We know this from the Psalms, many of which were sung. Now we can praise God with a perfect song of praise by way of singing in tongues. "I will sing with the spirit, and I will sing with the understanding also" (I Corinthians 14:15).

16. *A believer can bless with the spirit when he speaks in tongues.*
- I Corinthians 14:16

"...when thou shalt bless with the spirit..." (I Corinthians 14:6). This is another one of the many benefits of speaking in tongues. We can bless with the spirit. God sees speaking in tongues as a blessing!

17. Speaking in tongues is a means of giving thanks unto God.

‣ I Corinthians 14:16,17

"For thou verily givest thanks well…" (I Corinthians 14:17). This refers to praying in the spirit, which is speaking in tongues. The simple act of speaking in tongues does so much in the way of communication with God. What better way to extend our thankfulness to the heavenly Father than to utilize what He has given us to spiritually express our gratitude.

18. The apostle Paul spoke in tongues more than the Corinthian church.

‣ I Corinthians 14:18

"I thank my God, I speak with tongues more than ye all" (I Corinthians 14:18). No man since Pentecost has received the revelation of God's Word to the same extent as the apostle Paul. Certainly he would be an excellent example to follow. He evidently spoke in tongues much. Perhaps it would be a good idea for other believers to do likewise!

19. Speaking in tongues is a sign to unbelievers.

‣ I Corinthians 14:22

"Wherefore tongues are for a sign, not to them that believe, but to them that believe not: but prophesying *serveth* not for them that believe not, but for them which believe" (I Corinthians 14:22). This detailed explanation is directed to the church as a whole. It deals with those in the church who do not believe. They will realize that something special is occurring when they hear tongues and recognize it as a sign. Those who believe already know the significance of tongues and should be correctly operating the manifestation of prophecy instead.

20. *It is contrary to God's Word for someone to forbid the speaking of tongues.*
  ◆ I Corinthians 14:39

"Wherefore, brethren, covet to prophesy, and forbid not to speak with tongues" (I Corinthians 14:39). God explicitly says that no one should ever forbid anyone from speaking in tongues.

21. *Speaking in tongues should be done decently and in order.*
  ◆ I Corinthians 14:40

Speaking in tongues is done by the freedom of will of the speaker. He chooses if, when and where to do it. If the speaker wants to do unseemly activities while speaking in tongues, he can. It may be a disgrace to God, but he still can act by his own freedom of will. The believer should have enough love and respect to follow God's Word correctly. Believers should operate the manifestations decently and in order. Hopefully when the Christian grows in the true knowledge of God's Word it will become evident how precious speaking in tongues is and he will do it with great respect toward the heavenly Father.

God has provided an abundance of clear Scriptures to convincingly demonstrate exactly what speaking in tongues is. We have seen a multitude of benefits provided by speaking in tongues. By now, the significance of this wonderful manifestation of the spirit should be evident.

Today, there is little taught and less practiced regarding speaking in tongues. Yet, from a biblical perspective, as we have seen, speaking in tongues was designed to play a dynamic and necessary part in every believer's life.

Certainly the will of God is for believers to speak in tongues much. Why would God make something so dynamic and fulfilling if He did not desire His children to utilize it? I trust believers will heed the integrity of God's Word to learn to speak in tongues and then operate it daily in their lives.

CHAPTER SIX

Other Scriptures Pertaining to Speaking in Tongues

WE HAVE ALREADY HANDLED THE BIBLICAL RECORDS THAT obviously deal with speaking in tongues. Nearly all of the twenty-one different sections of Scripture we investigated use the words "speaking in tongues" to identify the subject as speaking in tongues. Now we will examine other verses in the Bible that refer to speaking in tongues. The following records do not literally use the words "speaking in tongues," but with the background of what we have already learned, we can see that the subjects of these verses point to speaking in tongues.

1. Praying in the spirit.

It became clear in our study of I Corinthians 14:14,15 that "praying in the spirit" or "praying with the spirit" referred to speaking in tongues (see # 16 of Chapter 4).

I Corinthians 14:14,15:
For if I pray in an *unknown* tongue, my spirit prayeth,
but my understanding is unfruitful.
What is it then? I will pray with the spirit, and I will
pray with the understanding also: I will sing with the
spirit, and I will sing with the understanding also.

It is obvious that speaking in tongues is referred to as "praying with the spirit" or "in the spirit." What a wonderful means of prayer God has designed! We can "pray with the understanding" and we can also "pray with the spirit," which is speaking in tongues.

As Christians we have a relationship with God Almighty. Most believers pray with their understanding, but when they learn of another aspect of prayer—that is, speaking in tongues—this should excite their soul. Speaking in tongues is, in a sense, "perfect prayer" because it is prayer in the spirit.

There are other sections of Scripture that use the phrase praying in the spirit, which could very well indicate speaking in tongues. Look at Ephesians 6:18:

Ephesians 6:18:
Praying always with all prayer and supplication in the
Spirit, and watching thereunto with all perseverance
and supplication for all saints.

The obvious question is: What is "prayer and supplication in the spirit"? From what we have already learned, a strong case could be made here that it refers to speaking in tongues.

Another verse using the term "praying in the Holy Ghost [holy spirit]" is Jude 20.

Jude 20:
But ye, beloved, building up yourselves on your most
holy faith, praying in the Holy Ghost.

This term "building up yourselves" through prayer in the spirit is very similar to I Corinthians 14:4: "He that speaketh in an *unknown* tongue edifieth himself...." The action of the spirit would be in a form of one of the nine manifestations that is designed to build up the believer, which most logically would be speaking in tongues. How wonderful for the believer to be built up.

2. *The spirit itself makes intercession for the believers.*

Romans 8:26,27:

Likewise the Spirit also helpeth our infirmities: for we know not what we should pray for as we ought: but the Spirit itself maketh intercession for us with groanings which cannot be uttered.

And He that searcheth the hearts knoweth what *is* the mind of the Spirit, because He [it] maketh intercession for the saints according to *the will of* God.

Verse 26 identifies our infirmity—"for we know not what we should pray for as we ought"—and continues by saying that the spirit itself (in manifestation) makes intercession for us. So the verse is talking about praying with the spirit in manifestation. We have already seen that God refers to speaking in tongues as praying in the spirit (see #1 earlier in the chapter). Speaking in tongues would be the logical manifestation referred to here. Earlier we read in Ephesians 6:18 that prayer in the spirit was being used for supplication for all saints. This also refers to speaking in tongues for others.

We may not always know what or how to pray, but when we speak in tongues, the spirit makes intercession for us and for the saints—those who are born again of God's spirit, according to the will of God.

People have been praying for others for many years, and now they can use the spirit of God in them by speaking in tongues to pray for others. What a wonderful lever of prayer!

3. The spirit gives witness that we are the children of God.

Romans 8:16,17:

The Spirit itself beareth witness with our spirit, that we are the children of God:

And if children, then heirs; heirs of God, and joint-heirs with Christ; if so be that we suffer with *him*, that we may be also glorified together.

How does the spirit bear witness with our spirit [inner being]? As we have already learned, the nine manifestations are the evidences of the spirit. We have already seen in our study that speaking in tongues was the manifestation given as a sign to indicate the presence of holy spirit abiding within (Mark 16:17; Acts 2:4; 10:45,46). These are some of the examples in God's Word showing speaking in tongues as being a sign or evidence of holy spirit being within us.

So when we operate the manifestation of speaking in tongues, it is the spirit bearing witness that we are children of God, heirs of God, and joint-heirs with Christ. What a wonderful truth to be reminded of every time we speak in tongues.

4. "…prayed for them, that they might receive the Holy Ghost: (For as yet he was fallen upon none of them)…" (Acts 8:15b,16a).

In this section of Scripture, we observe the results of Philip preaching to the Samarians. He had to deal with Simon who "used sorcery, and bewitched the people of Samaria, giving out that himself was some great one" (Acts 8:9). Philip had great results moving God's Word and many believed. Even Simon became born again.

But something was missing after the conversion of the people in Samaria, so the apostles Peter and John traveled to visit Samaria from Jerusalem. "Who when they were come down, prayed for them, that they might receive the Holy Ghost" (Acts 8:15). Why did Peter and John do this? Weren't the people in

Samaria already believers by way of Philip's teaching? "But when they believed Philip preaching the things concerning the kingdom of God, and the name of Jesus Christ, they were baptized, both men and women" (Acts 8:12). Yes, they were! Remember, it says even Simon believed. "Then Simon himself believed also…" (Acts 8:13). So why did Peter and John have to come down and pray for them to receive the holy ghost?

To answer this we need to first understand the context of this section of Scripture, then we need to understand the two Greek words representing the one English word "receive." First note verses 14 through 17:

> Acts 8:14-17:
> Now when the apostles which were at Jerusalem
> heard that Samaria had received [*dechomai*] the word
> of God, they sent unto them Peter and John:
> Who, when they were come down, prayed for them,
> that they might receive [*lambanō*] the Holy Ghost:
> (For as yet he was fallen upon none of them: only
> they were baptized in the name of the Lord Jesus.)
> Then laid they *their* hands on them, and they received
> [*lambanō*] the Holy Ghost.

From the context of this section of Scripture, we can observe that these Samarians had already believed. Peter and John's visit was not to give them more holy spirit; they already had it and could not get any more. There must be more to it than meets the eye. The key to understanding this is to realize that there are two different Greek words used for the one English word "receive." They each have specific meanings that will open our understanding greatly. *Dechomai* means "to receive or take hold of something with the purpose of having it." *Lambanō* means "to receive something in the sense of utilizing it."

Evidently, the people in Samaria had received the Word of God and believed it (v.14). Also, verse 12 indicates that they "were baptized, both men and women," indicating they had already received holy spirit. (Remember in Acts 1:5, Jesus told the disciples they would be "baptized with the Holy Ghost not many days hence," which meant they would receive holy spirit.) In other words, they had *dechomai*, received, the gift of holy spirit. But they clearly had not operated, *lambanō*, the manifestations of holy spirit.

So, Peter and John's concern was not that the Samaritans be born again, but why they had not manifested the holy spirit. In verse 15, the Word of God says they prayed for them to *lambanō* the holy spirit, which means to operate it.

"He was fallen upon none of them" (v.16). This is a figure of speech indicating that the spirit had not been manifested. They had already *dechomai* when they became born again. Now the concern was for the Samaritan believers to manifest the holy spirit they had received. So when verse 17 says, "they received [*lambanō*] the Holy Ghost" it means they operated manifestations, which most likely was speaking in tongues.

Up to this time in the young history of the Christian church, it was very normal and common for people to operate [*lambanō*] the manifestaions of holy spirit when they became born again. They would speak in tongues. Here in Samaria they got born again, but no one operated the manifestations. It was an important enough issue that they called in the top leaders of the church to minister. This deep concern by the church leaders plainly indicates the importance of speaking in tongues.

5. *We can sing in tongues, spiritual songs.*

> Ephesians 5:19:
> Speaking to yourselves in psalms and hymns and spiritual songs, singing and making melody in your heart to the Lord.

We have already learned from I Corinthians 14:15 that it is available to sing in tongues. "...I will sing with the spirit, and I will sing with the understanding also" (see Chapter 4, # 16). What a glory to God when we sing praises to Him! Even more, what a glory it is to the heavenly Father that we can now sing in tongues!

These other Scriptures pertaining to speaking in tongues add emphasis to the already established truth of the importance of speaking in tongues. Along with the twenty-one previous records examined, these other records support God's desire for his children to manifest the gift of holy spirit. He designed speaking in tongues to be utilized by the believer.

6. Worship in the spirit

Our heavenly Father is most deserving of our worship. It is He that has saved us from death and given us eternal life (Romans 6:23). We can worship Him as was done in the Old Testament, with singing, praising, giving thanks, and magnifying Him. Jesus Christ introduced a more preferred way of worshipping our God.

> John 4:23,24:
> But the hour cometh, and now is, when the true worshippers shall worship the Father in spirit and in truth: for the Father seeketh such to worship him.
> God *is* a Spirit: and they that worship him must worship *him* in spirit and in truth.

The Greek word used in John 4:23 and 24 for worship is *proskuneō* which means, "To prostrate one's self, do homage or reverence." It reflects the ultimate in showing respect. Another word rendered "worship" is *latreuō*. It means, "to serve or to do service." Philippians 3:3 is an example of where this word is used.

> Philippians 3:3:
> For we are the circumcision, which worship God in the spirit, and rejoice in Christ Jesus, and have no confidence in the flesh.

It is interesting to note that all the critical Greek texts read "worship by the spirit of God." How does one worship God by the spirit of God or worship God in spirit and in truth? The only logical way is via speaking in tongues. We have already seen the phrase "praying in the spirit," which indicates speaking in tongues. When we speak in tongues we are speaking directly to God (I Corinthians 14:2).

This makes so much sense when we consider the "true way of worshipping God." We cannot mess up speaking in tongues. The Old Testament is behind us and Jesus Christ taught us about true worship. What a blessing it must be for God to hear and see His children speak in tongues paying Him the homage He deserves.

7. *A sign of having entered into God's rest and refreshing because we have salvation through the complete work of Jesus Christ*

Speaking in tongues is a sign that we have Christ's salvation. We have rest and refreshing to our soul because we do not have to exert any effort to gain our salvation. As God's Word declares, "Not of works, lest any man should boast" (Ephesians 2:9).

Hundreds of years before Christ there was a prophesy given in Isaiah 28. This message was referred to by Paul in I Corinthians 14:21,22 to indicate tongues would be a sign of God's wonderful work through Christ.

I Corinthians 14:21,22a:
In the law it is written, With *men of* other tongues and other lips will I speak unto this people; and yet for all that will they not hear me, saith the Lord. Wherefore tongues are for a sign....

Isaiah 28:11,12:
For with stammering lips and another tongue will he speak to this people.
To whom he said, This *is* the rest *wherewith* ye may cause the weary to rest; and this *is* the refreshing: yet they would not hear.

Paul quotes Isaiah 28:11,12 to prove that tongues would be the rest and refreshing, as well as the sign of the Messiah who would come and finish the work of salvation for all mankind. In this section of Isaiah the leaders of Judah were ridiculing Isaiah for treating them like infants. They put their so-called righteous works before the Word of God. As a result of their unbelief the children of Israel could not enter into the rest God promised them.

God, through Isaiah, foretold that speaking in tongues would be a greater rest and refreshing. This would be the sign of the Messiah who would fully and completely do the work of salvation for us. Rev. Ken Petty puts this all together from his work: *More Than You all: The Power, Purpose and Profit of Praying in the Spirit.*

> We were being suffocated by sin, but now we can breathe again. Speaking in tongues is the proof that the times of refreshing have come in an individual's life. When we speak in tongues, we know that our salvation is not by our own works but by the works of God accomplished through Jesus Christ. We have ceased from our own works and entered into God's rest.

CHAPTER SEVEN

The Magnificence of Speaking in Tongues

WHY AM I SO EXUBERANT OVER THIS OBSCURED, HARDLY recognized act of speaking in tongues? The blunt answer is because it literally saved my life. Speaking in tongues gave me an assurance of my eternal relationship with God. It was the definitive answer to an eight-year-long prayer that started when I was twelve years old. As a result, I am ecstatic about speaking in tongues. This is the most exciting experience I have ever had.

Along with the twenty-one clear records in the Bible that deal with the evidence of speaking in tongues, there are other points of consideration that demonstrate the magnificence of speaking in tongues. In this chapter, we will witness a variety of experiences in God's Word as well as experiences resulting from God's Word that present the spectacular beauty of speaking in tongues.

These many marvelous accounts confirm to me the magnificence of speaking in tongues.

The First Century Church

The tremendous beginning of the Christian church occurred on the Day of Pentecost (Acts 2:1-4). It started with something new, dynamic, and very convincing. The twelve apostles were miraculously doing something totally impossible by their human ability. They were speaking in tongues! On this first day of the Christian church, they happened to speak in different languages which were recognized by the many visitors from countries all over the known world. These languages were unknown to the twelve apostles but easily recognized by the various foreign visitors. God chose speaking in tongues to highlight this most significant day.

On that first day of the Christian church, God introduced a whole new, never-before-used manifestation: Speaking in tongues. Jesus Christ said it would happen, and it did! (Mark 16:17). Speaking in tongues was selected by God to usher in the beginning of the Christian church that exists today in the lives of millions of people. The book of Acts displays several records of speaking in tongues being used and reveals its importance in the First Century Church.

How magnificent was the Day of Pentecost, when the twelve apostles first spoke in tongues! They were the first people to do so. Jesus Christ had instructed them of the greatness of what was to come, and now it was happening. This fantastic outpouring happened before thousands of people on the most significant of Jewish feast days. They must have been on fire! Peter's life was remarkably changed from hiding behind closed doors for fear of the Jews, to now out in the open preaching and accusing the Jewish leaders of their evil deed of crucifying the Lord Jesus Christ.

How precious it was for Cornelius, having searched diligently for the truth concerning God, to have an angel appear before him (Acts 10:1-46). He worshipped God the only way he knew. His diligence so impressed the heavenly Father that He sent an angel to give Cornelius, a Gentile, instructions to send for Peter in Joppa. At about that same time, God spoke to Peter to prepare his heart to receive the messengers from Cornelius. Culturally the Jews had no dealings with Gentiles. As a result of this, God had to work with Peter and show him a vision that communicated to him the acceptance of working with Gentiles. Peter finally got the point, traveled to Caesarea, and ministered to Cornelius and his household. They believed God's Word shared by Peter and received the gift of holy spirit. How did Peter and the other Jews that traveled with him know that Cornelius and his household had really believed and been born again? The undeniable proof is stated in the Bible: "For they heard them speak in tongues, and magnify God" (Acts 10:46). Peter and the Jews could not deny what had happened. They rejoiced at the reality that "God also to the Gentiles granted repentance unto life" (Acts 11:18).

How monumental it was that Paul responded to God's calling for his life. His conversion, as recorded in Acts chapter 9, does not mention Paul's speaking in tongues. But we know he operated the manifestation much in his life for he said, "I thank my God, I speak with tongues more than ye all" (I Corinthians 14:18).

How remarkable it was that the pagan city of Ephesus was opened to the movement of God's Word by Paul's helping twelve men to speak in tongues. They were already born again but had not manifested the spirit yet. Paul ministered to them by laying hands on them, "and they spake with tongues, and prophesied" (Acts 19:6). It must be noted that these men were saved at an earlier time by the ministry of Apollos, who unfortunately knew only "the baptism of John" (Acts 18:25). As a result of this, Apollos could not help them with manifesting the spirit via speaking in tongues. It took Paul's coming into Ephesus and correcting the teaching: "John verily baptized with the baptism of repentance, saying unto the people, that they should believe on Him which should come after him, that is, on Christ Jesus" (Acts 19:4). This new baptism was declared by Jesus prior to His ascension as recorded in Acts 1:4,5: "Wait for the promise of the Father.... For John truly baptized with water; but ye shall be baptized with the Holy Ghost [referring to the gift of holy spirit] not many days hence."

The act of speaking in tongues in the First Century Church as recorded in the Bible was the norm. There was no mistake on who was born again; they heard the believers speaking in tongues. Speaking in tongues was definitely important for the Christian walk, as evidenced by our heavenly Father devoting several chapters on the subject, as indicated in I Corinthians 12-14. The First Century Church set the example for future generations by being a spirit-filled church, speaking in tongues much.

My Experience with Speaking in Tongues

Why do I get so excited every time I speak in tongues? Every time I do, I am reminded that the Father is present with me. How incredible is that! Every time I speak in tongues, my heavenly Father, with all of His love, grace, mercy, and forgiveness, is present. The Scriptures say that God dwells in me as a born again one (I Corinthians 3:16).

As I continue to speak in tongues, I worship Him in spirit and in truth. I also am making intercession for the saints with perfect prayer to the Father. I am edifying myself spiritually as I speak in tongues. I know that I am a son of God and nothing can remove that reality from me.

It is inconceivable to me that anyone with the precious knowledge of God's Word would not want to speak in tongues and magnify Him.

If a child of God truly desires to worship God in spirit and in truth, he needs to speak in tongues. I am aware of worshipping the heavenly Father by way of music and praise songs, but there is nothing sweeter to His ears than to hear His children speaking in tongues. Music and words of prayer may sound heavenly to our ears, but speaking in tongues to God's ears is beyond the scale of measurement.

I never take speaking in tongues for granted. Really, it is a miracle every time I do it. I am speaking words of men or angels unknown to me, but for Him it is truly worship to His ears.

A Life-Saving Event

Speaking in tongues has affected my life in many ways through the years. One such event occurred when I was participating in a leadership training class in the mountains of New Mexico. We were caught high in the mountains unprepared for an unseasonal snowstorm in October. The rock climbing, rappelling, and long arduous hikes day and night were challenging enough, but now we faced a fierce storm.

We had been in New Mexico for about six days facing nothing but worsening, overcast, stormy weather. Every night the clouds obscured the night sky. A massive storm continued to move in that night. Later, we awoke to the collapse of our four-man tent. The snow had piled up on our tent to the point we were like an igloo with tent canvas as our inner walls. The feeling was claustrophobic; the ceiling was at my nose, leaving little room to move. The next night was similar to the previous with lots of snow covering our tents. It was this particular night that I awoke with the strangest feeling I think I have ever experienced. My mind was out of control with panic attacks.

I crawled out of my tent totally disoriented, not knowing what to do. Others in my tent just turned over and continued sleeping. For me, thoughts of fear and uncertainty were racing through my mind. I grabbed my mind and started speaking in tongues. Whenever I am faced with a challenging event, I have made it a practice to speak in tongues. Within seconds after speaking in tongues, I looked up into the sky to discover an opening large enough to identify a familiar star constellation. It was Orion. Remembering, that the Word of God is written in the stars (Genesis 1:14), I recalled the significance of this bright star group. Orion depicts the coming glorious one to conquer all. Speaking in tongues and seeing this awesome sign in the night sky assured my heart that I was safe. Within seconds the panic attacks subsided.

There is no situation in life that cannot be helped by speaking in tongues. God is not kidding us when He says, "I will never leave thee, nor forsake thee" (Hebrews 13:5).

Speaking in Tongue's Positive Effect on Our Brains

There have been several research studies by medical professionals as well as scientists that suggest benefits to the immune system during speaking in tongues. Other studies have indicated very interesting brain activity during speaking in tongues. A person can easily go on the internet and find these thought provoking studies. Those that I have found reveal fascinating observations. One seems to indicate the presence of some influence (spirit) causing the responses where there is no logical physical action taking place. As intriguing as these studies are, more studies are needed to verify or confirm the findings. Regardless, we know what God's Word says about speaking in tongues, and that we can be assured of.

Perhaps the most obvious positive effect speaking in tongues has on the brain is the fabulous feeling of knowing you are born again of God's spirit and that you have a proof that is undeniable. To know you are filled with Christ within, that you are heaven bound, and that all hell cannot stop you from going, definitely gives you a bounce in your step!

Knowing That Our Children Are Saved

Think how elated parents are when they hear their children speak in tongues confirming their eternal relationship with God. Three of the happiest days of my life were when I saw and heard my three children speak in tongues for the first time. I knew then, without a shadow of doubt that they belonged to the heavenly Father forever.

Every parent is excited to see their children walk as toddlers. As they grow up, we desire that they graduate from college and obtain a prosperous job. But isn't their spiritual success much more important than anything else? That is why, if parents knew God's Word regarding speaking in tongues, they would be thrilled at witnessing their children speaking in tongues for the first time. The assurance that their son or their daughter was heaven bound is beyond any other desire a parent could have pertaining to their children. They would now be comforted by the truth that their little one has an everlasting relationship with our loving heavenly Father.

How Significant Speaking in Tongues Really Is

Many of the finest moments in my life involve speaking in tongues. We live in a world that is filled with uncertainties. When I speak in tongues I know I am praying perfectly to my Heavenly Father. I am miraculously speaking a different language that blesses God. My heart is at peace. My prayer life is much more meaningful knowing how spiritually perfect speaking in tongues is. It has become second nature for me to utilize this powerful tool that God has given to me.

The loving act of praying for others is a very honoring event. The magnitude of this is demonstrated in Ephesians chapter 6.

At the end of Ephesians, God emphasizes the dire need for every Christian to put on the whole armor of God so that he can deal effectively with the devil.

> Ephesians 6:10-12:
> Finally, my brethren, be strong in the Lord, and in the power of his might. Put on the whole armour of God, that ye may be able to stand against the wiles of the devil.
> For we wrestle not against flesh and blood, but against principalities, against powers, against the rulers of the

darkness of this world, against spiritual wickedness in high *places*.

This powerful section of God's Word continues with the putting on the individual pieces of the armor. After putting on "the whole armor of God," a most important direction is given:

Ephesians 6:18:
Praying always with all prayer and supplication in the Spirit, and watching thereunto with all perseverance and supplication for all saints. [Biblically speaking "saints" includes all those who are born again of God's spirit].

"Praying always with all prayer and supplication in the spirit" is speaking in tongues, as indicated in previous chapters. Of all the things with which God could have closed Ephesians, He chooses the emphasis of speaking in tongues "for all saints." This is to be done with all "perseverance." The great act of the believer after standing fully fitted in his armor is speaking in tongues. We stand against the adversary by putting on the whole armor and praying in the spirit which is speaking in tongues. Speaking in tongues is really magnificent!

Now it is your turn to experience the profound greatness of speaking in tongues. Take God at His Word and recognize His desire for you to manifest the spirit that He has given you via the new birth. One of the most amazing experiences you will ever have is speaking in tongues the wonderful works of God!

CHAPTER EIGHT

Common Misconceptions and Fears about Speaking in Tongues

"WHAT IN THE WORLD WAS THAT STRANGE LANGUAGE?" This was my declaration upon hearing speaking in tongues for the first time. It sounded rather odd. This was a whole new spiritual experience for me. I was becoming very apprehensive to the idea of my speaking in tongues. As with anything that is new or that seems odd at first, it is quite normal to build up a fear against it.

Unfortunately, many misunderstandings have snaked their way into the minds of those who are looking into the manifestation of speaking in tongues. They most often stem from the fear of the unknown and from compromising the integrity of God's Word.

This chapter will be helpful in dispelling negative views of speaking in tongues. One minister from Great Britain wrote to me in response to reading the first edition of *Speaking in Tongues: A*

Biblical Perspective and said, "Tongues are generally looked down upon and are not spoken about or are regarded as some outlandish…over-the-top weirdo babbling." Unfortunately, there are many who have carried erroneous thinking about speaking in tongues into their Christian life. A careful investigation of God's Word should eliminate any fears or misconceptions about speaking in tongues.

Misunderstanding the Scriptures about speaking in tongues has formed a number of misconceptions and fears that discourage Christians from investigating this wonderful manifestation. If it were not for certain errors that have been promulgated through the years and produced unfounded fears, many believers would be experiencing an exciting, life-changing episode in their lives.

When I first heard about speaking in tongues and learned about its significance, several fears crept into my heart. These included: "Am I good enough before God to utilize this awesome manifestation?" "Was speaking in tongues really available to do after its origination some 2,000 years ago as recorded in the book of Acts?" There were some people who declared, "It went out with the first century apostles." There were even some well-meaning believers who said, "Such speaking of other languages was of the devil." These and other obstacles of misunderstanding have cheated many well meaning Christians away from manifesting one of the most rewarding abilities in Christianity.

The following are a number of misconceptions and fears that have thwarted the loving attempts of many Christians from manifesting one of God's most precious experiences. Many have been inundated with ideas from what other people have taught and not what the Bible teaches. We will use God's matchless Word to discover what our heavenly Father has to say about these concerns regarding speaking in tongues. The truth of God's Word dispels fear.

Psalms 34:4:
I sought the LORD, and he heard me, and delivered me from all my fears.

Many people call speaking in tongues a gift while God calls it a manifestation.

When we are born again, we receive the gift of holy spirit. Wrapped up in that gift are nine manifestations. These nine manifestations are not separate gifts, but they are evidences of the one gift of holy spirit.

An unfortunate problem in translations in the King James Version has caused people to call speaking in tongues a gift. In these verses: I Corinthians 12:1 and 14:1 and 12, the word "gifts" is used but they are italicized, which means it was added by the translators. There is no corresponding Greek word for "gifts" to be translated from. As a result of the additional word "gifts" in the KJV it has caused people to think speaking in tongues is a gift. As we will see, this is not the case. It is called a manifestation (I Corinthians 12:7).

The concept of calling the manifestation of speaking in tongues a gift ushers in the concern for people to question themselves, "Am I good enough to receive it?" Some people will say, "I am born again, but I have not received the gift of speaking in tongues." This is an incorrect understanding of the Scriptures. God is not a respecter of persons. Everyone who is born again receives the gift of holy spirit which includes all nine manifestations, including speaking in tongues.

I Corinthians 12:7:
But the manifestation of the Spirit is given to every man to profit withal.

The following verses contains a list of all nine manifestations.

I Corinthians 12:8-10:
For to one is given by the Spirit the word of wisdom; to another the word of knowledgeby the same Spirit;
To another faith by the same Spirit; to another the gifts of healing by the same Spirit;

> To another the working of miracles; to another
> prophecy; to another discerning of spirits; to another
> *divers* kinds of tongues; to another the interpretation
> of tongues:

The usage of the words "for to one" and "to another" refer to the words "to profit" in verse 7. This emphasizes that each one of the manifestations is to profit the person using them. In the next verse God puts it all together by saying: "But all these worketh that one and the selfsame Spirit, dividing to every man severally as he will" (I Corinthians 12:11). This verse confirms that all the manifestations stem from one spirit, and the person operates them as he wills. It is not saying, "as God wills," as some teach, but as the man wills, himself. God gives man freedom of will to utilize the spirit. God does not force any of the manifestations on an individual.

Because people mislabel speaking in tongues as a gift, they feel that God gives it only to certain deserving individuals.

Many believers fear that speaking in tongues is reserved only for the most deserving. Our loving heavenly Father makes a point in His Word to say that He is not a respecter of persons. "Of a truth I perceive that God is no respecter of persons" (Acts 10:34). He may be a respecter of conditions, such as when people believe, they receive, but He does not hold back from people to whom He has made His promises.

God has no favorites. He does not neglect some and favor others in giving what He has made available to all those who believe Him. We "all have sinned, and come short of the glory of God," it says in Romans 3:23. No one deserves, nor has earned the right to have, God's gift of holy spirit. Yet, Jesus Christ paid the price for every man on the face of the earth.

> John 3:16:
> For God so loved the world, that he gave his only
> begotten Son, that whosoever believeth in him should
> not perish, but have everlasting life.

The "whosoever" includes any and everyone. No one is excluded when it comes to the new birth. He loves everyone, and that is why there are no exceptions when it comes to the new birth and manifesting the gift of holy spirit.

> I John 4:13-15:
> Hereby know we that we dwell in him, and he in us,
> because he hath given us of his Spirit.
> And we have seen and do testify that the Father sent
> the Son *to be* the Saviour of the world.
> Whosoever shall confess that Jesus is the Son of God,
> God dwelleth in him, and he in God.

> Romans 8:9:
> But ye are not in the flesh, but in the Spirit, if so be
> that the Spirit of God dwell in you. Now if any man
> have not the Spirit of Christ, he is none of his.

What counts in life is to have the spirit of Christ in you. This comes as a result of believing upon the Son of God. Whenever anyone, regardless of who they are, confesses Jesus as Lord and believes that God raised Him from the dead, they are saved, born again, filled with the gift of holy spirit.

> Romans 10:9,10:
> That if thou shalt confess with thy mouth the Lord
> Jesus, and shalt believe in thine Heart that God hath
> raised him from the dead, thou shalt be saved.
> For with the heart man believeth unto righteousness;
> and with the mouth confession is made unto salvation.

They then have the capacity to speak in tongues. Just like the new believers did on the day of Pentecost when they declared, "We do hear them speak in our tongues the wonderful works of God" (Acts 2:11).

If God only allowed the "very good" to manifest speaking in tongues, then the apostle Paul would have never qualified. Paul consented to the death of Christians and had many put into prison. Yet, God forgave Him and allowed him to speak in tongues. "I thank my God, I speak with tongues more than ye all" (I Corinthians 14:18). Paul obviously recognized the value of speaking in tongues.

Some think that a believer may have to wait or "tarry" before they speak in tongues.

Many misled believers are taught that they have to wait for just the right time before God would have them experience speaking in tongues. This is a sad injustice to God's desire for every believer to speak in tongues right after they are born again.

The example in God's Word is that once people were filled with the gift of holy spirit, they manifested speaking in tongues immediately. On the day of Pentecost, they did not wait to manifest speaking in tongues. Cornelius and his family in Acts chapter 10 did not wait to manifest speaking in tongues. Our heavenly Father desires to hear you worship Him (Philippians 3:3), give Him thanks well (I Corinthians 14:17), and magnify Him (Acts 10:46). God's Word states, "I would that ye all spoke in tongues" (I Corinthians 14:5). He also declares that no one is to forbid anyone in speaking in tongues (I Corinthians 14:39). All of these together demonstrate a God who desires His children to operate the spirit given to them—without any waiting period.

Children are sometimes told not to speak in tongues until they are mature young adults.

Many who believe in speaking in tongues are hesitant to lead their children into speaking in tongues. They question whether they are capable of handling the spirit of God at a young age. God's Word does not say anything about age limits when it comes to manifesting the spirit of God.

For someone to be born again, they have to be able to understand who Jesus Christ is and what He did in redeeming mankind. They also have to grasp the concept of Jesus Christ being raised from the dead. The basic requirements for salvation are believing in the Son of God and making Christ Lord, as well as believing in the resurrection.

> Romans 10:9:
> That if thou shalt confess with thy mouth the Lord Jesus, and shalt believe in thine heart that God hath raised him from the dead, thou shalt be saved.

When a child is ready to believe in these realities, then they can take on having the gift of holy spirit abiding within. I have heard of five and six year olds manifesting the spirit. They must have been very mature for their age. One thing is for sure, we should not rush the process. They need to act on freedom of will. Once their understanding comes together, then they can get born again, walk by the spirit, and speak in tongues.

Some believe speaking in tongues went away with the close of the First Century Church.

The book of Acts reveals a vibrant and power-filled church that many say has never been repeated. Many have said that this was a unique time in history. All the miracles and healings—including speaking in tongues—were only for that period of time. This kind of thinking is erroneous. God's work did not end only in the First Century Church but has continued all through time to even now.

Today, people continue to be born again and do all the works of the holy spirit that were manifested in the First Century Church. I have personally witnessed and have been a part of many healings and miracles, and I have heard thousands of people speaking in tongues.

All through history, the Christian Church has witnessed all the signs, miracles, healings and other activities indicative of the power of God in manifestation. Included in these workings are speaking in tongues. In recent history speaking in tongues became very prevalent with the modern Pentecostal movement that started in Los Angeles in 1906. Hundreds of thousands of people speak in tongues today.

Some say speaking in tongues is placed last on the list of manifestations in I Corinthians 12 because it is least important.

This error is easy to defuse, because when a person opens their Bible and reads the listing they quickly find that it is listed second to the last!

> II Corinthians 12:10:
> To another the working of miracles; to another prophecy; to another discerning of spirits; to another *divers* kinds of tongues; to another the interpretation of tongues.

Whenever you have a list of items, something has to be last or second to the last. When people who adhere to this misconception happen to be from a large family and they are one of youngest children of the group, I like to make this point: "Since you were one of the last born in your family, are you least important?" This does not sit very well with those that are confronted with such logic.

Some think speaking in tongues is uncontrolled babbling.

People are fearful of hearing others speaking sounds they cannot understand. There have been a number of movies and even some documentaries that have shown speaking in tongues in an unfavorable light.

When speaking in tongues, the person maintains his or her freedom of will, so one can speak loudly or softly. They can fully control the process and stop and start at will.

One aspect believers need to be aware of is that God instructs born again ones to walk in love, operating the manifestations decently and orderly.

I Corinthians 14:40:
Let all things be done decently and in order.

The things of God are to be orderly and are not to bring confusion. A person who is speaking in tongues correctly will do so under control.

Some preach that speaking in tongues is of the devil.

The unusual behavior of some people while speaking in tongues has led others to declare that the act must be of the devil. Again, non-biblical movies and documentaries have shown speaking in tongues to be a matter of confusion. Then, to prove speaking in tongues is not biblical, they quote the Bible to say that God is not the author of confusion: "For God is not *the author* of confusion, but of peace, as in all churches of the saints" (I Corinthians 14:33). When people witness the confusion of people speaking in tongues, rolling around the aisles, and being "slain in the spirit," they attribute this all to the works of the adversary. The tongues are genuine, but the foolish acts are influenced by the devil.

Satan has worked overtime to discredit speaking in tongues and make it look ridiculous. God has given us freedom of will, so we are responsible for how we act while speaking in tongues. We need to remember what I Corinthians 14:20 states, "Let all things be done decently and in order."

Some are afraid they will get a counterfeit experience when speaking in tongues.

This is a common concern that people have when trying something new. When it comes to the operation of the spirit of God, our heavenly Father would not want us to experience anything counterfeit. One section of Scripture clearly declares this.

Luke 11:11-13:
If a son shall ask bread of any of you that is a father,
will he give him a stone? or if *he ask* a fish, will he for
a fish give him a serpent?

Or if he shall ask an egg, will he offer him a scorpion?
If ye then, being evil, know how to give good gifts
unto your children: how much more shall *your* heavenly Father give the Holy Spirit to them that ask him?

God would not give something evil to His son if he had asked for spiritual matters. This is true of any believer who approaches God to operate the manifestation. In your efforts to speak in tongues, go boldly to the throne of grace, knowing your heavenly Father would not give you anything but the best.

Some fear they might misuse the manifestation of speaking in tongues.

As we have already seen, God would not give us a counterfeit experience. We want to do our best for our heavenly Father, so we should learn the proper operation of the manifestations. If we make any mistakes, just remember that God is faithful to forgive us of our sins.

I John 1:9:
If we confess our sins, he is faithful and just to forgive us our sins, and to cleanse us from all unrighteousness.

We love God and He loves us and will work with us. Anyone with a loving, sincere heart that goes before the Father with a desire to bless Him will certainly manifest speaking in tongues correctly. We do our part in manifesting, which is moving our lips, throat, and mouth, pushing out the sounds. It is just like speaking in our native language, but we do not have to think what to say, because He does that. We just speak forth. By doing this we will not misuse this wonderful manifestation.

Some think they are not good enough before God to utilize the manifestations of holy spirit.

It is easy for man to think he can never be good enough to have the things of God. As Romans 3:11 says, "There is none righteous, no, not one." Everything we get from our heavenly Father is by grace. He loves us so dearly that He wants the best for us.

Our heavenly Father obviously loves us in spite of how sinful we were, because He sent His son to die for us so that we could have all the new birth qualities—including the gift of holy spirit and its manifestations. When He looks at us, all He cares to see is the fullness of Christ within. In the end, it is not how good we are, but it is how good God is to give us the fullness of the gift of holy spirit, along with the ability to speak in tongues and incorporate the other manifestations in our life.

Some people think speaking in tongues is the "gift of languages" so that they can become missionaries and speak the local language.

The whole idea of speaking in tongues is to pray in the spirit to the heavenly Father. There is nothing in God's Word that infers that people speaking in tongues would be sent out as missionaries to other countries.

Obviously, people who speak in tongues will probably have a strong prayer life and could be suited for missionary work. The fact that they do speak in tongues does not mean they will speak the language of the native people where they are sent. The only record of people understanding the tongues spoken is on the day of Pentecost, when those listening recognized their native language. God did this as a special blessing in introducing the receiving of the gift of holy spirit. At no other time did this ever happen as recorded in God's Word.

There are accounts of people hearing someone speaking in tongues and recognizing the language that was in tongues. They report that the language they spoke was with clarity and according to God's Word in content. Someone with a background of languages spoken in Iran commented that my tongue at that particular moment (I was working with her on manifesting speaking in tongues) was of a certain dialect from her country.

Some people associate speaking in tongues with being possessed by God and losing physical control of their bodies.

I have experienced being in a church service when all of a sudden people are babbling sounds and flopping about on the floor. This embarrassing scene happens all too often in certain churches that believe they are possessed by the spirit of God and give over their physical bodies to roll around and do all sorts of contorted movements.

The true God and Father of our Lord and Savior performs all things decently and in order. He expects us to do so, as well. I Corinthians 14:40: "Let all things be done decently and in order." God loves us and would never put us in awkward situations that would not bring glory to Him.

When someone speaks in tongues, it is by the freedom of will of that individual. They start and end when they so choose. The evil one tries to trick people into giving over their minds and bodies to his control. That is why someone may be speaking in tongues and yet possessed by the devil doing weird things. An example of this is when someone handles poisonous snakes while speaking in tongues. The tongue is probably genuine, but the handling of the snakes is either wrong teaching or devil spirit possession. As we operate this manifestation, our actions should be with the love of God.

There are some churches that handle snakes while speaking in tongues.

This is another situation where people do not renew their minds and therefore fill it with error about the proper function of speaking in tongues. In this case, they take literally what Mark 16:18 says, "They will take up serpents." They forget to read the rest of the verse that indicates that *if* they would do such an act by mistake, as the apostle Paul did in Acts 28:3-5 and was bitten by a snake, then they might not be harmed. The verse in Mark goes on to say, "And if they drink anything deadly, it will by no means hurt them." What is being communicated is that if a believer is bitten by a poisonous snake or drinks a contaminated liquid, that believer can be delivered unharmed.

The integrity of God's Word is always at stake. We must continue to be workmen of God's Word, rightly dividing it. In this case, the Scriptures were misunderstood and therefore misapplied, causing a most awkward error to occur. The sad result is that this turns many people off from speaking in tongues, because they do not want to be associated with snake handlers.

Conclusion

These misconceptions and fears should not hold the believer back from manifesting speaking in tongues. Once you recognize that God desires to hear from you via speaking in tongues, you will simply walk out and do it. There is absolutely no fear once God's Word is fully known. At that point, nothing will inhibit you from speaking in tongues.

CHAPTER NINE

The Benefits of Speaking in Tongues

ONE OF THE MOST NOTABLE MEN WHO HAS EVER LIVED IS quoted in the Word of God as saying, "I thank my God, I speak with tongues more than ye all," and, "I would that ye all spake with tongues," and, "forbid not to speak with tongues."(I Corinthians 14:18 and 5a, and 39b). This was the incredible apostle Paul who declared the importance of speaking in tongues. The indomitable apostle Peter also spoke in tongues and ministered this experience to others. Even the most important man of all, Jesus Christ, prophesied, "They shall speak with new tongues" (Mark 16:17).

Peter and Paul profited greatly by speaking in tongues. These two dynamic men of God, as recorded in the Scriptures, paint a moving example of what a significant role speaking in tongues played in their lives.

There are numerous benefits for the believer who speaks in tongues. This chapter presents a complete list, including comments, on how much speaking in tongues can affect the walk of a believer in a most profound way.

First, we will discover how Peter and Paul benefited immensely from speaking in tongues, then, we will witness the many benefits listed in God's Word of how speaking in tongues can benefit you, the reader.

THE APOSTLE PETER

The apostle Peter was one of the twelve disciples, when on that most significant day of Pentecost, they "…were all filled with the Holy Ghost, and began to speak with other tongues, as the Spirit gave them utterance" (Acts 2:4). At that time, there was quite an uproar with many thousands of people trying to understand what was really going on.

It took Peter, filled with the gift of holy spirit and having just spoken in tongues, to boldly stand before all the Judean leaders and everyone else that was visiting Jerusalem during this important feast celebration and to proclaim the truth.

What is most fascinating is that several days earlier Peter, along with the other disciples, were behind closed doors "where the disciples were assembled for fear of the Jews." (John 20:19). They thought they would be the very next ones to be crucified. Now, several days later, Peter is speaking in tongues, having been filled with the gift of holy spirit, and dynamically accusing the Judeans of their murderous crime.

> Acts 2:14 and 23b:
> But Peter, standing up with the eleven, lifted up his voice, and said unto them, Ye men of Judaea, and all *ye* that dwell at Jerusalem, be this known unto you, and hearken to my words:
> …ye have taken, and by wicked hands have crucified and slain.

Peter, fully inspired by the gift of holy spirit, is preaching without notes and preparation. Many people are hearing the message of salvation for the very first time. Jesus Christ crucified and raised from the dead is being boldly taught. The results are: "The same day there were added *unto them* about three thousand souls" (Acts 2:41).

What made the difference in Peter's life to change him from being full of fear and behind closed doors to boldly accusing the Judeans of murder? The only thing it could have been was Peter being filled with the gift of holy spirit and speaking in tongues. Jesus himself had told Peter and the other apostles that they would speak in tongues (Mark 16:17). Just before ascending on high, Jesus' last words were: "But ye shall receive power, after that the Holy Ghost is come upon you: and ye shall be witnesses" (Acts 1:8). The power they demonstrated was that they spoke in tongues. This occurred on the day of Pentecost.

Speaking in tongues was not a "one time" event. Peter was called by God to minister to the first Gentiles: Cornelius and his family. This record is in Acts chapter 10. Through a series of events, he traveled to minister to Cornelius and his household.

> Acts 10:44-46:
> While Peter yet spake these words, the Holy Ghost
> fell on all them which heard the word.
> And they of the circumcision which believed were
> astonished, as many as came with Peter, because that
> on the Gentiles also was poured out the gift of the
> Holy Ghost.
> For they heard them speak with tongues, and magnify
> God.

The apostle Peter was one of the most dynamic leaders to live in the Christian Church. God had Peter write the Word of God in what we have today as I and II Peter. It should be very clear that one of the most important things he ever did was speak in tongues. If speaking in tongues was beneficial for Peter, surely it will be good for us.

THE APOSTLE PAUL

The apostle Paul went from murdering Christians to becoming one. As a Pharisee he wielded great power and heavily persecuted the Christian Church. In Acts chapter 9, Jesus Christ came before him in a vision and changed his life. He became the great apostle Paul, who grew into becoming the most influential leader in the First Century Church. God had him write much of the New Testament, including Romans, Corinthians, Galatians, Ephesians, Philippians, Colossians, Thessalonians, Timothy, Titus, Philemon, and Hebrews.

Within the Word of God that Paul wrote, God directed him to declare, "I thank my God, I speak with tongues more than ye all" (I Corinthians 14:18). Obviously, speaking in tongues was very important to Paul. It helped make him the man of God he was. He, again through the inspiration of God, declared, "I would that ye all spake with tongues" (I Corinthians 14:5a). Later in writing the Word of God, he declared, "…forbid not to speak with tongues" (I Corinthians 14:39).

Not only is Paul recorded making these favorable statements about speaking in tongues, but he also was involved helping people to speak in tongues. In Acts chapter 19, Paul came to Ephesus finding some whom had not manifested the gift of holy spirit. They had been born again and had been filled with holy spirit, but they had not yet received it into manifestation. During the early Church it was normal for people to speak in tongues right after confessing Jesus as Lord and confirming their belief that God raised him from the dead. (Examples of this are on the day of Pentecost when they spoke in tongues and in chapter 10 when Cornelius' family spoke in tongues right away.) In this situation, as Paul arrived in Ephesus, it became evident they had not spoken in tongues. Paul in this case ministered to them, to help them speak in tongues.

Acts 19:6:
And when Paul had laid *his* hands upon them the
Holy Ghost came on them [The holy spirit came
upon them in manifestation. They were already born
again] and they spake with tongues, and prophesied.

The great apostle Paul spoke in tongues more than anyone else
and if he encouraged others to speak in tongues much, and if he
told the Christian Church not to forbid speaking in tongues. It
becomes quite evident to the Christian believer how vital speaking
in tongues really is.

Peter and Paul were the pillars of the early Church. Speaking
in tongues was an important part of their lives. It was a big deal
for them. If we are to model our lives after great men like Peter
and Paul, then speaking in tongues will be a most desirous action.

The one man every Christian person would want to emu-
late is Jesus Christ. Remember He told his followers that they
would be doing great signs and miracles, including speaking in
tongues (Mark 16:17). He also instructed the disciples on how
to manifest the gift of holy spirit. John 20:22 "…He breathed on
them [Instead of "on" it should be "in." The word "them" is italicized and is not in any of the critical texts] and saith unto them,
Receive [lambanō, meaning, To receive into action by using it]
ye the Holy Ghost:" What Jesus was doing was teaching them
how to receive the gift of holy spirit into manifestation when it
arrived. On the day of Pentecost, there was heavy breathing when
they first received the gift of holy spirit. They were breathing in
and it was then that they spoke in tongues. Another two verses
indicating Jesus taught his disciples about receiving into manifestation the gift of holy spirit are John 7:38 and 39:

John 7:38, 39:
He that believeth on me, as the scripture hath said,
out of his belly shall flow rivers of living water.

(But this spake he of the Spirit, which they that
believe on him should receive: for the Holy Ghost was
not yet *given*; because that Jesus was not yet glorified.)

The action of "out of his belly shall flow rivers of living water,"
turned out to be speaking in tongues. Jesus prepared his disciples
to operate this dynamic gift of holy spirit. If Jesus Christ was highly
in favor of speaking in tongues, so should every Christian believer.

You, too, can speak in tongues like Peter and Paul did.
Their example is proof enough of how speaking in tongues is so
dynamic and beneficial. Realizing Jesus Christ was very involved
in preparing his disciples to manifest the gift of holy spirit, which
was speaking in tongues, again speaks volumes of how valued
this God given manifestation was to our Lord and Savior.

BENEFITS OF SPEAKING IN TONGUES

You will discover that speaking in tongues is one of the most
exhilarating, soul satisfying acts you will do. As you learn the
many benefits of speaking in tongues, you will also rejoice in the
privilege God has set before the Church that they could have
such a beautiful means of communicating with Him and praying
for others.

To know that you are a child of God and a joint heir of Jesus Christ

No greater feeling have I ever experienced than realizing I
was born again, a child of God and a joint heir with Jesus Christ.
When I spoke in tongues for the first time, I knew without a
shadow of a doubt that I belonged to the heavenly Father. There
was no denying it because I was speaking in tongues.

Speaking in tongues was proof enough for the apostle Peter
and his Judean followers that Cornelius and his family, in spite of
being Gentiles, were born again. They heard them speak in tongues.
They could not deny the concrete proof of speaking in tongues.

Romans 8:16,17a:
The Spirit itself beareth witness with our spirit, that
we are the children of God:
And if children, then heirs; heirs of God, and joint-
heirs with Christ.

The only act of the Spirit bearing witness with our spirit
is speaking in tongues. What a wonderful reality our heavenly
Father has put into place! We can have proof of the spiritual reality of being a son of God and a joint heir with Christ.

To edify or build you up

One of the great benefits of speaking in tongues is that it
edifies you. I cannot count the many times my heart would be
troubled and I would speak in tongues and be encouraged. The
world is always trying to tear us down. God's manifestation of
speaking in tongues is always there to build us up.

I Corinthians 14:4a:
He that speaketh in an *unknown* tongue edifieth
himself.

Jude 20:
But ye, beloved, building up yourselves on your most
holy faith, praying in the Holy Ghost [which means
speaking in tongues].

To speak to God directly and speak divine secrets

People today want to talk directly to God and they want to
hear from Him. This is exactly what speaking in tongues does. It
is the spirit in you speaking to God.

I Corinthians 14:2:
For he that speaketh in an *unknown* tongue speaketh not unto men, but unto God: for no man

understandeth *him*; howbeit in the spirit he speaketh mysteries [divine secrets].

How incredible is our heavenly Father to allow us to speak mysteries or divine secrets with Him. That is exactly what the above verse is declaring. We have direct access to God Almighty. It is our spirit talking to God who is Spirit (John 4:24).

To speak the wonderful works of God

God's Word declares that when we speak in tongues, we are speaking the language of men or angels (I Corinthians 13:1). The speaker does not know what he or she is saying, but God has designed it that he or she is speaking the wonderful works of God. We are not speaking wasteful words of gossip or other nondescript words, but we are speaking the wonderful works of God. How loving it is of our heavenly Father to allow us to speak this way.

> Acts 2:11:
> Cretes and Arabians, we do hear them speak in our tongues the wonderful works of God.

To magnify God

When a person wants to express himself to someone he really loves, he may come to find it difficult to come up with the appropriate words. We love our heavenly Father so much and desire to say just the right words to praise Him. When we speak in tongues, we are speaking words that magnify Him. What a privilege we have to express ourselves in the best manner possible by speaking in tongues.

> Acts 10:46:
> For they heard them speak with tongues, and magnify God.

To pray perfectly

There are many times we do not know what to say in prayer. Our infirmity is that we just can't come up with the correct words to say. When we speak in tongues, our prayer is perfect because it is that perfect spirit from God praying. We are so fortunate to have this lever of prayer when we pray for others and come before the Father. It is the spirit that makes intercession for us according to the will of God. That has to be perfect, because the spirit of the perfect God gives us the words to speak through the spirit abiding in us.

> Romans 8:26,27:
> Likewise the Spirit also helpeth our infirmities: for we know not what we should pray for as we ought: but the Spirit itself maketh intercession for us with groanings which cannot be uttered.
> And he that searcheth the hearts knoweth what *is* the mind of the Spirit, because he maketh intercession for the saints according to *the will of* God.

To worship God truly with the spirit

There are a number of ways in the Old Testament that God was worshipped. These include singing, praising, giving thanks, and magnifying Him, to name just a few. Jesus Christ in the New Testament introduced another preferred way of worshipping God.

> John 4:23,24:
> But the hour cometh, and now is, when the true worshippers shall worship the Father in spirit and in truth: for the Father seeketh such to worship him.
> God *is* a Spirit: and they that worship him must worship *him* in spirit and in truth.

According to E.W. Bullinger in *Figures of Speech Used in the Bible*, the words "in spirit and in truth" in verses 23 and 24 are figure of speech called hendiadys, in which two words are used but only one thing is meant. Bullinger translates verse 24: "They that worship God, who is spirit, must worship Him with the spirit, yes – really and truly with the spirit."

How can a person worship God with the spirit? The only way logically is speaking in tongues. We have already seen the phrase "praying in the spirit," which indicates speaking in tongues. When you speak in tongues you are speaking not unto men but to God (I Corinthians 14:2). Other Scriptures within this chapter indicates speaking in tongues magnifies God, gives thanks well to God. It makes sense that to worship God with the spirit would have to be speaking in tongues. Philippians refers to worship in the spirit.

> Philippians 3:3:
> For we are the circumcision, which worship God in
> the spirit, and rejoice in Christ Jesus, and have no
> confidence in the flesh.

People talk about doing worship services, which usually means singing or praising. This is nice, but what really pleases our heavenly Father is worshipping Him truly in the spirit which is speaking in tongues.

To give thanks well

The more I learn of God's awesome love for us, my heart pours out with appreciation. What more thanks can I express than to use what He has given to me? What touches the heart of a parent is to observe their children utilizing the gifts that we give them. This is so true with the heavenly Father. Someone once said, "God's heart melts when He hears us speaking in tongues."

> I Corinthians 14:15,17:
> I will pray with the spirit, and I will pray with the
> understanding also….
> For thou verily givest thanks well, but the other is not
> edified.

Verse 15 helps us see that verse 17 is connected with praying in the spirit, which is speaking in tongues. The least we can do is speak in tongues much giving Him thanks well.

To have the Spirit bearing witness with our spirit

The one action God designated to demonstrate that the spirit is in us is speaking in tongues. God did not leave the spirit-filled believer without any tangible witness of His presence in us. The spirit bearing witness with our spirit is speaking in tongues.

> Romans 8:16:
> The Spirit itself beareth witness with our spirit, that we are the children of God.

We have the assurance of knowing the spirit of God resides in us. Hearing yourself speak in tongues verifies in your heart the spiritual realities of what God's Word declares. You have the proof that is undeniable. It matches up to the Word of God.

To make intercession in your prayer life for situations and for the believers

This aspect of speaking in tongues is astounding. We can get a picture of someone in our mind and then speak in tongues for them. It is perfect prayer in the spirit for others. There may be a situation you do not know what is going on, but there is a concern and need for prayer. Instead of worrying about trying to find out what is going on, we just pray in the spirit or speak in tongues and it is covered. God is so gracious by allowing us to just speak in tongues and then He does the rest.

> Romans 8:26,27:
> Likewise the Spirit also helpeth our infirmities: for we know not what we should pray for as we ought: but the Spirit itself maketh intercession for us with groanings which cannot be uttered.
> And he that searcheth the hearts knoweth what *is* the mind of the Spirit, because he maketh intercession for the saints according to *the will of* God.

Ephesians 6:18:
Praying always with all prayer and supplication in the
Spirit, and watching thereunto with all perseverance
and supplication for all saints;

The power of this kind of prayer is magnified in the above verse in Ephesians 6:18. Reading the context of this part of God's Word we witness that we are in a spiritual battle. "For we wrestle not against flesh and blood, but against principalities, against powers, against the rulers of the darkness of this world, against spiritual wickedness" (Ephesians 6:12). The next several verses are the encouragement to "take unto you the whole armour of God" (Ephesians 6:13). What is so remarkable is that, after putting on all the pieces of the armor, the one great act we do is pray in the spirit, which is to speak in tongues. This is how immensely powerful manifesting speaking in tongues is!

To be a sign to unbelievers

Unfortunately today, when people hear someone speak in tongues, they question, "What is this weird activity?" This is how bad our world has gotten. For those who are hungry for the truth, it will pique their curiosity to check it out. For those who will not believe, this will seem crazy. For those who will believe, it is a sign of the spirit of God in manifestation.

I Corinthians 14:22:
Wherefore tongues are for a sign, not to them that
believe, but to them that believe not: but prophesying *serveth* not for them that believe not, but for them
which believe.

Mark 16:17:
And these signs shall follow them that believe; In my
name shall they cast out devils; they shall speak with
new tongues.

Acts 2:11:
Cretes and Arabians, we do hear them speak in our
tongues the wonderful works of God.

Jesus Christ declared that the sign to look for would be speaking in tongues (Mark 16:17). People ought to listen to our Lord and Savior and heed His words. When the visitors to Jerusalem witnessed these Galileans speaking their language, it perked up their soul and got them to listen.

To give a rest and refreshment to the soul, because it is a sign of having salvation in Christ

Hundreds of years prior to the day of Pentecost, it was prophesied that there would be a language spoken that would sound like stammering lips. The results of people speaking like this would actually bring a rest and a refreshing to the soul.

Isaiah 28:11,12:
For with stammering lips and another tongue will he
speak to this people.
To whom he said, This *is* the rest *wherewith* ye may
cause the weary to rest; And this *is* the refreshing: yet
they would not hear.

Paul refers to this Isaiah record while writing I Corinthians 14:21,22.

I Corinthians 14:21,22a:
In the law it is written, With *men of* other tongues
and other lips will I speak unto this people; and yet
for all that will they not hear me, saith the Lord.
Wherefore tongues are for a sign....

The record in Isaiah was a prophesy foretelling that speaking in tongues would be the rest and the refreshing. Paul was demonstrating this truth in I Corinthians 14:21,22. What was occurring during Isaiah's time was that the leaders of Judah were ridiculing Isaiah for treating them like children. They were promoting their works above God's. As a result of their unbelief, the children of Israel could not enter into the rest God promised them.

Today, speaking in tongues is the proof to the believers that they have made Jesus Lord of their lives and have entered into God's rest. They have ceased from their own works trying to reconcile themselves back to God and have recognized the full and complete salvation work of Jesus Christ on their behalf. As a result of God's grace and mercy they have entered into the family of God. As believers speak in tongues they are reminded of this and therefore have the rest and refreshing of God.

To bring a message from God (or, when interpreted, for God) to a group of people

Speaking in tongues is a part of another manifestation that brings an edifying message to the listeners, to comfort or exhort them. The following verses demonstrate what exactly this wonderful manifestation does and how it is to operate in the Church.

> I Corinthians 14:5,13,27:
> I would that ye all spake with tongues, but rather that ye prophesied: for greater *is* he that prophesieth than he that speaketh with tongues, except he interpret, that the church may receive edifying.
> Wherefore let him that speaketh in an *unknown* tongue pray that he may interpret.
> If any man speak in an *unknown* tongue, *let it be* by two, or at the most *by* three, and *that* by course; and let one interpret.

The purpose of the manifestation of prophesy is similar to the purpose of the manifestation of tongues with interpretation.

If someone speaks in tongues in a meeting, that person should interpret the message as God gives them the interpretation. The message is not for the individual, but solely for the body of believers as they fellowship and meet together. This manifestation of prophecy builds up the listeners with its message as does the manifestation of interpretation of tongues.

To experience possible health benefits

There have been several research studies that suggest benefits to the immune system during speaking in tongues. Other studies have indicated very interesting brain activity during speaking in tongues. As intriguing as these studies are, more studies are needed to verify or confirm the findings. I would not be surprised to find that such benefits are true—they certainly fit with what God's Word states—but they would only be one small part of the benefits of speaking in tongues.

The assurance of knowing you are born again of God's spirit and that you have a proof that is undeniable, brings a mental health that can't help but give a person a wonderful feeling. To know you are rich with Christ within and you are heaven bound—and all hell cannot stop you from going—definitely gives you confidence and peace.

Conclusion

It is amazing how much speaking in tongues benefits the believer. Peter and Paul spoke in tongues much and experienced its benefits in their ministries. Jesus Christ would not have foretold of speaking in tongues unless there was a significant purpose for it (Mark 16:17).

My prayer is that believers will experience the many astounding benefits of speaking in tongues. My prayer is that through speaking in tongues they will experience the reality of knowing they are children of God and joint heirs with Jesus Christ; that they will be edified; that they realize they are speaking directly to God and speaking divine secrets to Him; that they know they are speaking the wonderful works of God; that they know they are magnifying the Father; that they are praying perfectly; that they are giving thanks well; that they realize they have the witness of the spirit within; that they can make intercession in their prayer life for situations and for other people; that they show themselves to be a sign to unbelievers; that they have the rest and refreshing to their souls; that they can also operate the manifestation of tongues with interpretation; and that they experience possible health benefits. May the truth of God's Word prevail in your life. May you speak in tongues much!

CHAPTER TEN

How to Speak in Tongues

INTRODUCTION

ONCE THE WORD OF TRUTH HAS BEEN RIGHTLY DIVIDED, IT becomes evident that the manifestation of speaking in tongues is a valuable resource for the believer.

It is amazing to consider what the heavenly Father did throughout the ages to bring about the greatest gift He has ever offered—holy spirit. It is so precious that it cost God His only begotten Son. There has never been a more valuable price paid for anything. God's love and desire to bless mankind is beyond comprehension, and yet there it is, written clearly in His Word. God, to mark the greatest gift man has ever received, used something new, something so clear and obvious that no one could miss the realization of having holy spirit within. He provided the manifestation of speaking in tongues.

The workman of the Word of God can clearly observe that Jesus Christ declared speaking in tongues would be a sign of the indwelling gift of holy spirit. When God first made the new birth available with the gift of holy spirit on the day of Pentecost, He marked it with the operation of the manifestation of speaking in tongues. This, along with the many other verses we have covered, demonstrates the magnitude of speaking in tongues. God certainly made it a very significant act. Now the informed believer can utilize this dynamic manifestation by learning to speak in tongues.

Logically, to manifest speaking in tongues should be one of the deepest desires in the heart of a believer. The following points, which have already been covered in this study, are some of the many reasons why a person would desire to speak in tongues.

Reasons to Speak in Tongues

- To be able to confirm in your heart that you are truly born again of God's spirit.
- To be able to prove that you are a child of God, heir of God and joint heir with Christ.
- To be able to talk directly to God.
- To be edified spiritually.
- To be able to pray in the spirit.
- To be able to bless with the spirit.
- To give thanks to God via the spirit.
- To speak mysteries, divine secrets.
- To speak the wonderful works of God.
- To magnify God.
- To make intercession for the believers.
- To give witness that we are the children of God.
- To sing spiritual songs.
- To worship God in the spirit.
- To experience the rest and refreshing to your soul because we have the redemption in Christ.

LEARNING TO SPEAK IN TONGUES

Having had the opportunity to help hundreds of people through the years to speak in tongues, I would like to offer the following suggestions that will be helpful for you, the reader, to speak in tongues.

1. Learn about God's salvation plan—which He wrought through Jesus Christ—through a knowledge of God's Word, so you can be born again (or saved) as outlined in Romans 10:9. Jesus Christ is the way, the Truth and the life (John 14:6). There is no other name under heaven whereby you must be saved (Acts 4:12).

   Romans 10:9:
   That if thou shalt confess with thy mouth the Lord Jesus, and shalt believe in thine heart that God hath raised him from the dead, thou shalt be saved.

2. Learn what God's Word teaches about speaking in tongues and build a desire to do it. Build into your heart a confidence and a trust in what God's Word says about speaking in tongues.

3. Realize while you are seeking that God would not give you a counterfeit. God loves you and as our heavenly Father He only wants the best for you.

   Luke 11:11-13:
   If a son shall ask bread of any of you that is a father, will he give him a stone? Or if *he ask* a fish, will he for a fish give him a serpent?
   Or if he shall ask an egg, will he offer him a scorpion?
   If ye then, being evil, know how to give good gifts unto your children: how much more shall *your* heavenly Father give the Holy Spirit to them that ask Him?

THE ACTUAL DOING IT

1. Understand the mechanics of speech. Realize what it takes to speak physically, then apply this to speaking in tongues. The believer has to move his or her lips, mouth, and throat and say the words. God is not going to use you like a puppet and force words out of your mouth. You have the freedom of will to speak or not to speak. God is always there with the words for you to utter when you speak forth.

2. Realize that God does not possess or force you to speak in tongues automatically. You have to initiate the process with your desire by opening your mouth and forming the words.

   When I first learned to speak in tongues, there was one thing that held me up. I was waiting for God to move me. I soon learned that I could not wait for God to push me over the cliff, so to speak. You take the initiative to just start speaking sounds, keep it going, and do not stop. You have to form the words and give it the push so it comes out. God will not do it for you.

3. Freedom of will always applies to speaking in tongues. The believer has to will to do it.

   You do not have to wait for God to move you to speak in tongues. You can do it any time you desire. That is what so wonderful about it. We have the freedom of will. We have to take the initiative and say the first word regardless of how it sounds. Then we keep it rolling.

   It is very important, when you first speak in tongues, to do it a lot. Some people will do it a little and stop and then get talked out of it by the adversary, saying, "Did you really do it?" Step out and just speak forth the sounds. It will sound strange and very different. If you have ever heard foreigners speak around you, you would say their language sounds odd. So it is when you first speak in tongues. Jesus Christ taught His disciples about manifesting holy spirit when they would receive it in the future (John 7:38,39).

John 7:38,39:
He that believeth on me, as the scripture hath said, out of his belly shall flow rivers of living water. (But this spake he of the Spirit, which they that believe on him should receive: for the Holy Ghost was not yet *given*; because that Jesus was not yet glorified.)

Once you speak, keep on speaking for a long period of time. Remember, you are talking to God, magnifying Him, giving thanks unto Him, worshipping Him and more.

4. Speak out boldly. You take the first step in moving your mouth, lips, and throat to give the words. You do not need to think about what words to speak. God is always there. Just move your mouth and speak out loud boldly.
   If at this point, you have not spoken in tongues by now, then take a rest and then start over. This time, take your time and go over each step carefully. It would help to ask someone who is experienced in helping other people, to assist you. If you cannot find someone to work with you, then you are welcome to contact me at 619-223-3032 and leave your name and phone number.

I encourage you to take God at His Word and speak in tongues. Be blessed in all the fullness of what God has made available through His gift of holy spirit. He wants you to speak in tongues, so be patient and persistent in your endeavors to speak in tongues.
Nothing brings more real peace to the soul than to speak in tongues. Knowing the significance of speaking in tongues, you

will want to speak in tongues often. One of the greatest places to speak in tongues is in your car while driving alone. You can speak out loud, you can sing in tongues to your favorite tune. Remember, speaking in tongues is for your private prayer life. It is not designed for speaking out loud in front of others. Many people say their spiritual life really takes off once they are speaking in tongues. For me, there is nothing more awesome than to speak in tongues.

CHAPTER ELEVEN

Some Final Words

ONE OF THE MOST EXHILARATING TIMES IN MY LIFE TOOK place on a summer night in the middle of a cow pasture in Ohio. As I gazed up in the clear evening sky, the tears in my eyes gave more sparkle to the stars above. My thoughts were flooded with thankfulness to my newly found heavenly Father. My mouth was producing words of a language I knew not. But, without a doubt, I knew I was operating a manifestation of holy spirit born within me. I was speaking in tongues. I was experiencing a dream come true. I had a desire to know that I really knew that God was alive and I had a permanent relationship with Him. Now, for me, there was no shadow of a doubt, because I was speaking in tongues. I knew I was born again of incorruptible seed, I had Christ in me; I was a child of God; I had eternal life and the hope of Christ's return. Nothing could be more satisfying to my soul then to have this reality confirmed in my heart. I was doing something that was naturally impossible to do, and yet, because God's spirit was inside me, I was speaking in tongues.

Speaking in tongues is the God-provided proof of the internal reality and presence of the gift of holy spirit within the Christian. God gives the ability to speak in tongues to every man or woman who is born again.

I trust this work reflects a dedicated exercise of being a workman of God's Word. I have endeavored to rightly divide the Word of Truth. I believe anyone who is meek and hungry to learn, and who cares for the integrity of God's Word, can embark on a wonderful adventure through the Scriptures and find gems of truth.

I made a point of not quoting any other work (except the research books for word definitions) to support this project. The point was not to take a stand on some belief, but to simply see what the Scriptures say. This presentation is certainly not an exhaustive study on speaking in tongues. It does, however, provide a basic working of the subject to provide a foundation for deeper study.

Speaking in tongues, as we have clearly seen, is one of the great realities God has purposed for his children to do. Why so many Christians miss this significant truth is a testimony to the lack of care for the integrity of God's Word. It has been disheartening to see the negative attitudes that so many people have toward speaking in tongues. I trust this work will draw attention to the simplicity of working God's Word and provide a proper exposure to a subject that can be such a tremendous blessing to the believer.

Certainly we have observed with this simple overview of the Scriptures that speaking in tongues is a spiritual reality of great value and significance. God, in His love and grace, has provided an undeniable means to confirm the new birth of the believer. What a wonderful privilege to be able to talk directly with God, to magnify Him, and to give Him thanks—all because we can speak in tongues!

My prayer for the reader is that he or she can clearly see for him or herself the accuracy of God's Word regarding the benefits of speaking in tongues. I pray that everyone who truly hungers to operate the gift of holy spirit by speaking in tongues will do so.

> I Corinthians 14:2a:
> For he that speaketh in an *unknown* tongue speaketh not unto men, but unto God.

Acknowledgments

Nothing of significant value exists without recognizing God, the heavenly Father, and His Son, Jesus Christ. God, in His infinite mercy and love, allowed man to be. He provided the best possible relationship by way of His Son, the Lord Jesus Christ. Without their manifested love, speaking in tongues—or anything else God provided man—would be of little value. So, first and foremost, I thank the heavenly Father for His love and guidance to be able to produce this work.

There have been many people who have provided their love, support, encouragement and expertise in my life. I cannot remember and name them all, but God knows and remembers their labor of love and will reward them accordingly.

There are a few people I would like to acknowledge. Jeanie, my wife of more than twenty-seven years, has been my partner and soul mate. She is one of God's greatest gifts to me. Our three children, Tim, James, and Suzanne, are all answers to prayer. They love God and support the work of the ministry and have been a major source of encouragement and love. They will each make noteworthy contributions to the body of Christ.

I thank the faithful believers in San Diego who have blessed my life immensely so that I could take on this project. There are a number of fellow workers who have been instrumental in suggesting, supporting, reviewing, and critiquing the work as it progressed. Warren and Vikki Barnhart, Barbara Bennett, David Bergy, Wayne Clapp, Jill Eisenstein, Bob Falk, Ken Fonda, Susan

Propst, David Setzer, and Mike Tomberlin provided their expertise in biblical insight and/or advice in grammar. I am especially indebted to Dr. Victor Paul Wierwille, whose work in biblical research and teaching on the manifestations of holy spirit is most noteworthy.

2nd Edition Acknowledgements

A nucleus of people helped with the second edition. Bob Falk has been and still is one of the key people on this project. His encouragement, suggestions, and proofing were indispensable. He has been a faithful friend from the very beginning. Jerry Corridi became the English teacher I am glad I never had. His critical notes and insight to grammar made me feel like I was failing English 101 all over again. I am immensely grateful for his valuable time. Ken and Darlene Petty helped more than they can ever imagine. Ken's keen ability in biblical research provided great insight on some of the aspects of speaking in tongues. Jeanie, the wife of my dreams and the most beautiful proofreader in the world, tirelessly gave of her time and energy. Many others, who were mentioned in the first edition, helped along the way. Thanks to everyone else that I failed to mention, for being part of a project to help make speaking in tongues one of the most understood and used resource in Christianity.

BIBLIOGRAPHY

Bach, Marcus. *The Inner Ecstasy*. New York: Abingdon Press, 1969.

Berry, George R. ed. *The Interlinear Greek – English New Testament*. Grand Rapids, Michigan: Zondervan Publishing House, 1971.

Bullinger, E. W. *A Critical Lexicon and Concordance to the English and Greek New Testament*. Grand Rapids, Michigan: Zondervan Publishing House, 1975.

Companion Bible, The. E. W. Bullinger, Grand Rapids, Michigan: Kregel Publications, 1990.

Dillow, Joseph. *Speaking in Tongues: Seven Crucial Questions*. Grand Rapids, Michigan: Zondervan Publishing House, 1975.

Douglas, J. D., ed. *The New Bible Dictionary*. Grand Rapids, Michigan: Eerdmans Publishing Company, 1962.

Geer, Christopher C. *Walking in God's Power® Foundational Class Student Study Guide*. Stirling, Scotland: Word Promotions Ltd., 1995.

Geer, Christopher C. *Walking in God's Power® Intermediate Class Student Study Guide*. Stirling, Scotland: Word Promotions Ltd., 1995.

Hagin, Kenneth E. *Tongues: Beyond the Upper Room*. Tulsa, Oklahoma: RHEMA Bible Church, 2007.

Hagin, Kenneth E. *Why Tongues?* Tulsa, Oklahoma: Kenneth Hagin Ministries, 1975.

Holy Bible. American Revised Standard Version 1901, Camden, New Jersey: Thomas Nelson & Sons, 1929.

Kelsey, Morton T. *Tongue Speaking*. Garden City, New York: Doubleday and Company, 1964.

Kittel, Gerhard, ed. *Theological Dictionary of the New Testament*. Grand Rapids, Michigan: Eerdmans Publishing House, 1983.

Manetti, Ren. *In the Church, Prophecy Is Equal to Speaking in Tongues Plus Interpretation*. Lancaster, California: Our Biblical Heritage Press, 2000.

McDougal, Harold. *Speaking in Tongues: Understanding the Uses and Abuses of This Supernatural Phenomena*. Hagerstown, Maryland: The McDougal Publishing Company, 1988.

Metz, Donald S. *Speaking in Tongues: An Analysis*. Kansas City, Missouri: Nazarene Publishing House, 1974.

Meyer, Joyce. *Filled with the Spirit*. Fenton, Missouri: Faith Words, 2002.

Moulton Harold K. *The Analytical Greek Lexicon Revised*. Grand Rapids, Michigan: Zondervan Publishing House, 1978.

Newberg, Andrew. *Why We Believe What We Believe*. New York, New York: Free Press, 2006.

New Testament in Four Versions. Christianity Today, Inc., New York: The Iverson-Ford Associates, 1963.

Petty, Ken. *Lessons in Dynamic Christian Living: Introductory Bible Study*. Oracle, Arizona: Dynamics of Christian Living Press, 2006.

Petty, Ken. *More Than You All: The Power, Purpose, and Profit of Praying in the Spirit*. Oracle, Arizona: Dynamics of Christian Living Press, 2013.

Roberts, Oral. *The Baptism with the Holy Spirit and the Value of Speaking in Tongues Today*. Tulsa, Oklahoma, 1966.

Rice, John R. *Speaking with Tongues*. Murfreesboro, Tennessee: Sword of the Lord Publishers, 1968.

Sherrill, John L. *They Speak with Other Tongues*. Grand Rapids, Michigan: Baker Book House, 1964.

Strong, James. *Strong's Exhaustive Concordance of the Bible*. Nashville, Tennessee: Royal Publishers, 1979.

Unger, Merrill F. *New Testament Teaching on Tongues*. Grand Rapids, Michigan: Kregal Publications, 1971.

Webster's Seventh New Collegiate Dictionary. Springfield, Massachusetts: G. & C. Merriam Company, Publishers, 1972.

Wierwille, Victor Paul. *The New, Dynamic Church*. New Knoxville, Ohio: American Christian Press, 1971.

Wierwille, Victor Paul. *Power For Abundant Living*. New Knoxville, Ohio: American Christian Press, 1971.

Wierwille, Victor Paul. *Receiving the Holy Spirit Today*. New Knoxville, Ohio: American Christian Press, 1982.

Wigram, George V. and Winter, Ralph D. *The Word Study Concordance.* Wheaton, Illinois: Tyndale House Publishers, 1978.

Young, Robert. *Young's Analytical Concordance to the Bible.* Nashville, Tennessee: Thomas Nelson Publisher, 1982.

Zodhiates, Spiros. *Speaking in Tongues and Public Worship.* Chattanooga, Tennessee: AMG Publishers, 1997.

Speaking in Tongues: A Biblical Perspective
Order Form

Postal orders: **Robert Lindfelt**
P.O. Box 6008
San Diego, CA 92166

Contact info: **619-223-3032**
office@sdbiblicalstudies.com

Please send *Speaking in Tongues: A Biblical Perspective* to:

Name: _____

Address: _____

City: _____ State: _____

Zip: _____

Telephone: (_____) _____

Book Price: $12.00

Shipping: **$3.00 for the first book and $1.00 for each additional book to cover shipping and handling within US, Canada, and Mexico. International orders add $6.00 for the first book and $2.00 for each additional book (send check or money order to Robert Lindfelt).**

or contact your local bookstore
or Amazon.com

Wholesale bookstore discount price list available upon request.